P9-CFT-133

*f*P

ALSO BY JAMES L. KUGEL

Great Poems of the Bible

The Bible As It Was

On Being a Jew

The Idea of Biblical Poetry

In Potiphar's House

THE GOD OF OLD

Inside the Lost World of the Bible

JAMES L. KUGEL

THE FREE PRESS

New York Toronto London Sydney Singapore

THE FREE PRESS
A Division of Simon & Schuster, Inc.
1230 Avenue of the Americas
New York, NY 10020

Designed by Leslie Phillips
Manufactured in the United States of America

2 4 6 8 10 9 7 5 3 1

LIBRARY OF CONGRESS CATALOGING-IN-PUBLICATION DATA IS AVAILABLE

Kugel, James L.
The God of old ; inside the lost world of the bible / James L. Kugel
p. cm.
Includes bibliographical references and index.
1. Bible. O.T.—Criticism, interpretation, etc. 2. Bible. O.T.—Theology
3. God—Biblical teaching.
BS1192.6 .K84 2003
2002045592

ISBN 0-7432-3584-3

There is none like unto the God of Jeshurun, who rideth upon the heavens in thy help, and in His excellency on the sky.

The eternal God [or: God of Old] is thy refuge, and underneath are the everlasting arms: and He shall thrust out the enemy from before thee; and shall say, Destroy them.

Deut. 33:26–27, King James Version

FOR R.

CONTENTS

ABOUT THIS BOOK

The Hebrew Bible was composed over an extended period. More than a thousand years separate its earliest and latest parts. During this long period, people's understanding of God naturally changed.

We know a great deal about how God was conceived toward the end of the biblical period, since that way of thinking is in many ways still with us. This is the God inherited by later Judaism and emergent Christianity, and thus, in many ways, is the God of our religions today. But what of earlier times, what of the God of Old?

Archaeology, ancient Near Eastern history, and biblical scholarship have filled in some of the background of those early times. Scholars nowadays are well aware that the God of ancient Israel first existed in a world of many gods; it was only after a long process of development that the idea of monotheism—that there is only one divine power in the universe—came to be widely accepted. Along with this, scholars have also noted that some of our most basic assumptions about God—that He has no body but exists everywhere simultaneously, that He is all-knowing and all-powerful—are not articulated in the most ancient parts of the Bible.

But if that is so, what did it mean to believe in the God of Old? What did ancient Israelites actually understand Him to be, and how did they conceive of His interaction with them?

Such questions can be disturbing. We like to think that what our religions say nowadays about God is what people have always believed. Even biblical scholars sometimes shy away from the implications of their scholarship when it comes to these basic questions. "We really cannot know much," some say, "about what ancient prophets or ordinary Israelites thought they perceived about God—God as they knew Him." Along with this goes an unspoken second objection: what good would it do if we could? Surely biblical faith, at its earliest stages, was a primitive thing; much of what people believed then would only embarrass us now.

I have undertaken to write this book because I believe that what ancient Israelites perceived can indeed be discovered: the evidence may be found within the Bible itself. As for the second objection, I think that it is likewise in error. The things that are examined in this book are not all of one piece. The ancient narratives in which angels appear to various biblical figures are very different from the "starkness" passages characteristic of certain psalms and prophecies, and these passages are themselves quite distant from legal texts that forbid the making of divine images or invoke the odd concept of the "cry of the victim." Taken together, however, these different texts seem to share a common theme, about the interpenetration of the domains we like to separate under the headings of "spiritual" and "material." It is not that ancient Israelites could not conceive of such a separation, but rather that it did not appear to them absolute and inviolable—on the contrary, ordinary reality was constantly in danger of sliding into something else entirely, something stark and eerie and nonetheless familiar. This is a theme that, considered in its fullness, could hardly be described as primitive. On the contrary, the God of Old has something to tell us not only about where our faith came from, but about its most basic reality today.

THE GOD OF OLD

1
The Project

My field is the study of ancient texts. I have spent the better part of my life working on them, mostly texts from the Hebrew Bible, the Dead Sea Scrolls, and other writings of the ancient Near East, but also Hebrew texts from the middle ages. One thing I have learned through my years of studying is that authors, although they are writing on some specific topic and for some definite purpose, often end up telling more than they set out to. Especially if a text is of any length or substance, it can open a window onto the inner world of the person who wrote it, revealing something crucial about how that person saw and understood things in general. Such information is often far more valuable than whatever it was the author had consciously set out to write about. The reason is that the author himself, and all the things he thought were obvious or took for granted, are by now long gone. The text is the only thing we have that will allow us to enter that lost world and, with some effort, restore its way of understanding, of *seeing*. The trick, of course, is to know how to allow a text to tell everything it knows about its author and his world.

This afternoon, I was in the library studying a poem written by a Hebrew poet of the middle ages. It is a poem about the soul, and reading it, I thought again of the Project. People in medieval times had such a vivid sense of their own souls! We often accuse ourselves nowadays of self-absorption, self-obsession, and there is more than a little truth to this. But in medieval times, even though the self in which they were absorbed was quite different, people were as aware as we are today, perhaps even more so, of what was going on deep inside themselves. They sometimes said that they felt their soul was "sick" and needed tender caring. They said they felt it, *felt* it, crying out in distress. Like a lovesick maiden (though, one might add, with the intensity of a dog chained to a stake), it was sobbing and moaning in its frantic desire to be reunited with its Creator. Some of this may have been literary convention, poetic boilerplate, but behind that must have been a certain reality in their world that has disappeared from our own. I thought of the dusty treatises I had once consulted, with their prescriptions for the soul's care and betterment, a diet of devotion and medicinal herbs, proper readings, and a path of penitence to bring the soul back to its native strength.

Outside the library, one comes to one's senses: the traffic, the brightly lit stores. But still, always lurking, is the Project. What is the Project? It is not mine in particular; many people have worked at it. Perhaps it began for me at the time of the Vietnam War, or perhaps even before that. Events conspire to put you on the spot, to cause you to make some fateful decision. And just then, facing life's ugly, jagged teeth, you suddenly feel a certain calm and a sense of the realness of things that isn't there most of the time, the realness of yourself as one distinct person, and certain ideas go through your head. A few years pass, perhaps. Then, on a day that you have set aside, sitting alone on a park bench above some municipal lake, you try to smooth things out in your mind, until the surface of the lake subtly starts to seem like an image of your mind, and once again you have a different sense of things. It is then that the Project can present itself most forcefully, reemerging from wherever it may have been waiting. The Project is: to get to the bottom of this, to see how far it goes; not to deceive oneself, not to be sentimental or weak, but to see how far one can go.

It can take you very far, even fill up a lifetime. Oddly, for me, it led eventually to (among other places) a most unlikely setting, the library. The reason is implied in what I have already said. I did not invent the idea of the soul, or of God, I was not the first to write about Him. Those who were, and those who followed them, lived long ago, and now all that remains of their world is those texts that they left behind. At first they seem so dry and dead, but if they are read in the right way—with sympathy and imagination, no condescension, only a relentless desire to enter—they can indeed come back to life, and their world, their way of seeing, can let us in to take the measure of things that are strange.

2

The Moment of Confusion

> And it came to pass, when Joshua was in Jericho, that he lifted up his eyes and saw, and behold! A man was standing across from him with his sword drawn in his hand. So Joshua went up to him and asked, "Are you one of us or one of our enemies?" And he answered, "Neither. But I am the chief of the LORD's army; I have just arrived." Then Joshua fell facedown to the ground in prostration and said to him, "What does my lord wish to say to his servant?" And the chief of the LORD's army said to Joshua. "Take your shoe from off your foot, for the place upon which you are standing is holy"—and Joshua did so. (Josh. 5:13–15)

Angels are a fairly common feature in biblical narratives. Various factors made their existence a necessity in ancient times. One of them was that biblical narratives did not like to speak of God actually appearing to human beings directly and conversing with them face-to-face. The reason was not that God in those days was thought to be invisible, and certainly not that He was (as later philosophers and theologians were to claim) altogether spiritual and therefore had no body to be seen. Rather, God in the Bible is not usually seen by human beings for an entirely different reason, especially in the earliest parts: catching sight of Him was believed to be extremely dangerous. "No man can see Me and live" (Ex. 33:20). Therefore, when God wished to speak to people, He normally did so by sending an angel, that is to say, a humanlike stand-in. The most common Hebrew word for "angel" *(mal'ākh)* seems to come from a root meaning "send"—and this would confirm the general impression that scholars have of the angel's role in the Bible's most ancient parts. An angel, it would seem, was essentially an emissary used by God to represent Him among human beings. (The same word, *mal'ākh,* was sometimes used of ordinary, human messengers, such as those sent by Jacob to his brother in Gen. 32:3.) So it seems to be with Joshua in the above-cited passage: this "chief of the LORD's army" appears to be a representative, or messenger, of God who suddenly appears to Joshua.

In the passage quoted, it is difficult to tell what the purpose of this emissary's visit might have been. Perhaps it was simply to tell Joshua that he is standing on holy ground, or perhaps we are meant to understand that the divine message that follows in the next chapter (Josh. 6:2–5) is the continuation of the words spoken here by the "chief of the LORD's army." Whichever the case, what strikes me as crucial in this passage is the moment of confusion that the biblical narrative has taken the trouble to report. "Are you one of us or one of our enemies?" Joshua asks, thinking that the man he has just now seen is an ordinary person. Joshua is, of course, afraid: normally people don't come at you with their swords drawn. But perhaps, he reasons, this man is actually one of his own troops or some allied fighter—hence, apparently, his nervous question. All this is to say that, at least at first glance, the "chief of the LORD's army" must have looked altogether like a regular human being. As soon as Joshua is told the truth, however, he falls down in abject obeisance and waits for further instructions.

An angel, one would think, should be recognized easily enough. Yet, interestingly, this moment of confusion seems to come up a great deal in biblical narratives about angels. Here is an extended example from the book of Judges:

> There was a certain man from Zorah, a Danite by the name of Manoah, whose wife was barren and had borne no children. Now, the angel of the LORD appeared to the woman and said to her: "Though you are barren and have not borne, yet you shall become pregnant and give birth to a son. But you must be careful not to drink wine or strong drink, nor may you eat anything impure. And after your pregnancy, when you give birth to a son, no razor shall touch his head, for the boy will be a nazirite of God from the time of his birth—and it is he who will begin to save Israel from the Philistines." Then the woman went and told her husband, "A man of God [that is, a prophet] came to me, but he looked very frightening, like an angel of God, so I did not ask him where he was from, and he did not tell me his name. But he did say, 'You will become pregnant and bear a son—but do not drink wine or strong drink and do not eat anything impure, because the boy will be a nazirite of God from the time of his birth to the day of his death.' "
>
> Then Manoah prayed to the LORD and said: "O my Lord!

Let the man of God whom You sent come again to us and instruct us what to do for the boy to be born." God heeded Manoah's prayer and the angel of God returned to the woman while she was sitting outside, but her husband Manoah was not with her. So the woman quickly ran back and told her husband and said, "That same man is back who came to me the other time." Manoah went and followed his wife until he came to the man, and asked him, "Are you the man who spoke with my wife?" and he said, "Yes." Manoah said, "If what you said is true, then what are we supposed to do with the boy?" The angel of the LORD said to Manoah, "Let your wife be careful about everything I told her. She must not eat anything that comes from grapevines, nor drink wine or strong drink, nor eat anything impure—she should make sure to do everything that I told her." Manoah said to the angel of the LORD, "Permit us to detain you and kill a goat for you[r dinner]." The angel of the LORD said to Manoah, "Though you detain me I will not be able to eat your food; but if you wish to make a burnt offering to the LORD, then send it up"—because Manoah did not realize that he was an angel of the LORD. Then Manoah said to the angel of the LORD, "What is your name? For, when what you said comes true, we will want to honor you." The angel replied, "Why should you be asking about my name, since it cannot be known?" Then Manoah took the goat and the grain offering, and offered them up to the LORD on a rock, and something wondrous happened while Manoah and his wife were watching. As the flames were rising up from the altar toward the sky, the angel of the LORD rose up in the flames of the altar. And Manoah and his wife saw this, and they fell on their faces to the ground.

The Moment of Confusion

> The angel of the LORD never again appeared to Manoah and his wife; thus, Manoah understood that it was an angel of the LORD. And Manoah said to his wife, "We will surely die, because we have seen God." But his wife said to him, "If the LORD wanted to kill us, He certainly would not have accepted the burnt offering and grain offering, and He would not have shown us all these things, in fact, He would not let us be hearing this now." And the woman gave birth to a son and called him Samson. (Jdg. 13:2–24)

How interesting that this narrative has gone out of its way to stress the moment of confusion. In fact, here it is no moment but an extended period of time. Manoah's wife (unnamed in the story) clearly thinks her visitor is a "man of God." This is one of the terms used in the Bible for a prophet, and indeed, it is easy to understand her confusion. After all, she has encountered a being who appears altogether humanlike, and if he has announced that her barren womb will soon be opened and has further instructed her about preparing her future son to be a nazirite to God (a type of ascetic in ancient Israel: see Numbers 6 and 1 Samuel 1), she draws the logical conclusion: the person to whom she was speaking must indeed have been some sort of prophet foretelling the future. Her husband, Manoah, then asks God to send the man of God back again, and when he reappears, what Manoah's wife says only seems to underline the couple's confusion. "That same *man* is back who came to me the other time," she announces, and Manoah then asks him. "Are you the *man* who spoke with my wife?" Apparently, this God-sent messenger looks very much like an ordinary person (although we are meant to remember the first impression of Manoah's wife, namely, that the stranger appeared "very frightening, like an angel of God"—he is not altogether ordinary looking). We, of course, appreciate the irony; the narrator has already said that this actually is an angel, and, as if to stress that fact, the narrator then repeats that it is "the angel of the Lord" whom Manoah invites to share a meal with his wife and himself. But they perceive nothing unusual. Apparently, it was a well-known fact that angels do not eat or drink, so to the reader/listener, the angel's response to Manoah's invitation is altogether comprehensible: I cannot eat the animal you propose to serve me, so perhaps you should offer it as a sacrifice instead. Such a response ought to have tipped off the hospitable couple as well, but it does not. They seem to be in some sort of fog. Instead, they just go ahead as instructed and prepare a sacrifice.

By this point the narrative tension is almost unbearable: we know what is happening, but poor Manoah and his wife are still in the dark. When will they figure it out? Even the angel's cryptic response to their request to know his name—"Why should you be asking about my name, since it cannot be known?"—does not seem to trigger any response in them; apparently still in a fog, they simply shrug it off and go on with their preparations for the sacrificial offering. It is only when the angel ascends to heaven on the flames of the altar that Manoah and his wife finally understand, and then their reaction is identical to that of Joshua above: they fall down on the ground in prostration.

This is reminiscent of yet another encounter with unrecognized angels, this one involving Abraham in the book of Genesis.

> The Lord appeared to him [Abraham] at the oak-trees of Mamre, as he was sitting near the door of his tent during the hot part of the day. He looked up and saw three men standing

near him. As soon as he saw them he ran from the tent-door to meet them, and bowed to the ground. "Gentlemen," he said, "if you please, do not, I pray, just pass your servant by. Let a little water be brought so that you can wash your feet and rest underneath this tree. Then I will fetch a bit of bread so that you may satisfy your hunger before resuming your journey—after all, you have come this way to your servant's place." They replied, "Do just as you have said."

Then Abraham hurried into the tent to Sarah and said: "Quick! Knead three *seahs* of choice flour and make some loaves." Next, Abraham ran to the cattle and chose a calf, nice and tender, which he gave to the servant-boy to prepare quickly. After that, he took curds and milk, along with the calf that had been prepared, and set them out before them. Then he stood by under a tree while they ate.

They said to him, "Where is your wife Sarah?" and he answered, "In there, inside the tent." Then one said, "I will be back this time next year, and your wife Sarah will have a son." Sarah had been listening at the door of the tent, which was in back of him. Now Abraham and Sarah were old, well advanced in years; Sarah had stopped having the periods that women have. So Sarah laughed to herself, saying, "After I am all used up will I still have relations—not to mention that my husband is old too!" Then the LORD said to Abraham, "Why did Sarah laugh, saying, 'Can I really give birth, old as I am?' Is anything too much for the LORD? I will be back this time next year, and Sarah will have a son." (Gen. 18:1–14)

What is interesting is that in this narrative—unlike the incident with Manoah and his wife—we are never really told that

Abraham has understood who his visitors are. The passage begins by asserting that "the LORD appeared" to Abraham—but this assertion seems to come from the narrator's point of view. What Abraham sees is "three men standing near him," and his exaggerated courtesy and zeal in preparing a meal for his unannounced guests seems intended simply to show what a generous host he is—it is no indication that Abraham has somehow figured out his visitors' secret identity.* Indeed, later interpreters of the story liked to stress that Abraham had no idea whom he was serving. (One such interpreter was the New Testament author of the letter to the Hebrews, who draws the following lesson from Abraham's behavior: "And remember always to welcome strangers, for by doing this, some people have entertained angels *without knowing it*"—Heb. 13:2.)

In any event, just like Manoah and his wife, Abraham wishes to feed the visiting strangers, and they agree to eat (or at least to pretend to). Their gruff answer to Abraham's invitation—"Do just as you have said"—might have tipped Abraham off that these were no ordinary visitors, but he seems to notice nothing unusual. He tells Sarah and the servant boy to prepare the food without mentioning who these guests are; apparently, he himself has no idea. Even their question, "Where is your wife Sarah?"—how do these strangers know his wife's name?—seems to arouse no curiosity in Abraham. Like Manoah and his wife, Abraham seems to be in some sort of fog. As in the previous example, the

* To be clear, I am not assuming that this story, like the previous one, presumes that angels do not eat. I only mean that his generosity ought not to be interpreted as a sign that he has understood who his visitors really were—the point, on the contrary, seems to be that he was gratuitously generous.

moment of confusion here is much more than a moment: it is apparently dragged out throughout the strangers' meal. But in the end, the truth does seem to have dawned on the couple, for when God* says to Abraham, "Why did Sarah laugh? . . . Is anything too much for the LORD?" Sarah immediately denies it "because she was frightened" (Gen. 18:15). If she is frightened, it would seem that she has figured out with whom she is speaking. But not much is made of this—the moment of recognition here (if that is what it is) certainly seems to receive less attention than the moment of confusion that precedes it.

The question I wish to consider is: why was this moment of confusion important? It certainly could have been omitted from the brief passage about Joshua, and there was scarcely any reason to stress it so obviously in the story of Manoah and his wife or of Abraham and Sarah. The fact that it is important, that the narrator actually goes out of his way to make sure that the reader understands that these various biblical figures took a while to realize what was going on, is quite undeniable, however. It would appear, then, that this is one of those cases when a text seems to be telling us—perhaps even inadvertently—something important about its own world. But what is the significance of this moment of confusion?

Modern biblical scholars have not been unaware of this feature in biblical narratives, and some have suggested that it indeed has a discernible purpose: verisimilitude. It is, they say, as if the narrator were telling us, "This was no daydream or hallucination. So-and-so actually did see such an angel; in fact, it was so

---

* Note: "the LORD" and no longer the three men.

real looking that he thought it was actually a man." But I must say that this explanation seems weak, even counterproductive, in the passages examined thus far. After all, if the being that Joshua saw really looked so much like an ordinary man, perhaps that was all he was—an enemy soldier with a sword in his hand, but one who, having stumbled into Joshua's field of vision, had the presence of mind to claim to be "chief of the LORD's army" and so avoid a potentially nasty confrontation with the Israelite general. If that was what happened, wasn't Joshua a fool for believing him and falling to the ground! In other words, from the narrator's standpoint, it would have been much better to describe the angel in altogether nonhuman terms, elaborating the supernatural details accompanying his appearance—the strange aura surrounding him or, perhaps, the sparks and flames shooting forth from his sword—thus leaving no doubt in the reader's mind that this unworldly encounter really did take place. Nothing was to be gained by implying that the angel looked humanlike; indeed the opposite would seem to be true.

The situation is still more difficult to understand in the case of Manoah's wife. After all, the woman is suffering from a "closed womb"—who is to know if it is she or her husband who is responsible for her infertility? Under those circumstances, suggesting that she encountered someone who looked like an ordinary man, and that this encounter took place (quite anomalously for the biblical world!) when she was alone, was simply to open the door to the suspicion that the man himself was responsible for the sudden termination of her barrenness, and that all the rest was simply her (or the narrator's) cover story. Certainly, no biblical author would have wanted even to raise such a suspicion. So why mention this angel at all? Let the woman be told in some other way that her barrenness is about to end. Or if there must be an angel, why does the text not mention something—anything—supernatural about his appearance, or at least announce his arrival in some supernatural way? But in all three of the stories we have examined, it seems simply to be a given that angels are not recognized as such, at least at first. Indeed, as we have seen with both Manoah and Abraham, people seem extraordinarily obtuse, in a fog, when confronted by an angel, so that the oddest sort of speech or behavior is simply shrugged off. Only after a while comes the moment of recognition, and then—just as odd, when you think about it—those who have previously been in a fog react with surprise *but not incomprehension.* Apparently, everyone knows what an encounter with an angel is like and, at least after the angel's identity is revealed, how to behave in such a situation.

❀ ❀ ❀

Angels are a peculiarly Israelite phenomenon in the ancient Near East. Mesopotamian gods sometimes have envoys and servants, but they do not function with human beings in the same way as the angels seen above, and they certainly play no important role. Nevertheless, the moment of confusion is far from unique to the Bible. In the writings of many peoples, gods come down to earth disguised as human beings or animals—as, for example, Zeus, Athena, and other gods and goddesses do in Greek epic. Often the disguise passes undiscovered, but sometimes there is the same sort of wavering confusion seen above. Consider, for example, this appearance of the goddess Venus to her own mortal son Aeneas in Virgil's *Aeneid:*

His mother appeared to him standing along the way in the midst of the forest. She had a girl's face and clothes, and even carried the weapons of a girl from Sparta (though she might otherwise have looked like Harpalyce the Thracian, who outruns horses and can go faster than the winged river Hebrus). Like a hunting-girl, she had a bow hanging handily from her shoulder, and she let her hair blow loose in the wind. The top part of her garment was gathered with a knot, leaving her knees bare. "Hey, you fellows," she said [to Aeneas and his companions]. "Tell me, have you by chance seen a sister of mine wandering near here? She would have on a spotted lynx-skin, with a quiver on her belt, and be chasing and shouting after some foaming wild boar." So spoke Venus. Then the son of Venus [Aeneas] began his reply: "I have not heard or seen anything of your sisters— Say, how should I be calling you, young maiden? For you really don't have the face of a mortal, nor does your voice sound human . . . Certainly you're a goddess, then. A sister of Apollo? Or maybe someone from the nymph family? Anyway, whoever you are, please be kind and give us a hand—tell us what skies we are under now, and on which of the world's shores we have been cast. For we are wandering about without knowing the people here—or the place; we were driven here by wind and huge waves. We will offer many sacrifices upon your altars."

Then said Venus: "Oh, I am hardly worthy of any honor such as that [given to the gods]! Girls from Tyre usually carry a quiver and wear these dark red hunting boots tied at the top."

Venus then begins her long answer to Aeneas's question, explaining that he is in the Tyrian city of Carthage, in Africa, and telling him about Dido, ruler of the place. At the end of their exchange, she tells him to take heart and continue on his way.

> She spoke, but as she turned away, a glint of rose shone forth from her neck and her heavenly hair exhaled its godly perfume. Her garment now flowed down to her very feet, and by her demeanor she was revealed to be a true goddess. Now he recognized his mother and pursued her with these words as she vanished: "Why do you cruelly delude your own son with disguises? Why not have our hands clasp each other and have our voices speak and reply in truth?" With such words he reproved her, then headed off toward the walls of the city. (*Aeneid* 1:314–37, 402–10)

What Aeneas sees, at least at first, is a beautiful young woman. Virgil's vaguely erotic description of her clothing, along with the repeated insistence on her being a young maiden, is meant to tell us that Aeneas at first looked at her with the eyes of many a young man beholding an attractive young woman for the first time. Indeed, his almost-first words to her—*o quam te memorem, virgo?*—belong more to the world of singles' bars than divine-human encounters: "By the way, honey, what's your name?" But almost from the start he becomes aware that something else is going on—she must be a goddess, he says. Yet this does not seem to strike Aeneas as particularly crucial, and Venus, for her part, denies it: "I'm just a regular Tyrian girl," she says. Aeneas does not argue the point, and although he seems to sense that something is afoot, it is only at the end of their long conversation that he finally understands that he has actually been speaking to his own mother. Then, of course, he is vexed—she ought really to have told him straight off (and come to think of it, why didn't she?)—vexed but not flabbergasted or even, truly, surprised.

Behind this little encounter stands a world of conventions from ancient Greece and Rome that is altogether different from that of ancient Israel—gods who beget humans, gods who turn themselves into humans, gods who turn humans into other people or animals or things, and so forth. It would certainly be unwise simply to equate this passage with the biblical ones seen above. At the same time, it would be foolish to overlook the similarities. It may well be that behind Virgil's passage—behind even the literary conventions on which it is based—stands a reality that is indeed comparable to the one that we have been surveying in the biblical context, even if the focus is less single-mindedly on the moment of confusion. In that world too, divine creatures present themselves to human beings in such a way that they are not recognized, at least not at first—and then sometimes, as with Aeneas and Venus, something clicks.

ↄ ↄ ↄ

Another biblical moment of confusion:

> The angel of the Lord came and sat beneath the oak-tree in Ophrah, which belonged to Joash the Abiezrite, while his son Gideon was beating out grains of wheat in the winepress to keep them safe from the Midianites. The angel of the Lord appeared to him and said, "The Lord is with you, you mighty warrior." Gideon said to him, "Excuse me, sir, but if the Lord is with us, why are we having all this trouble? Where are all the miracles that our ancestors recorded for us, saying, 'Truly, the

LORD took us up out of Egypt'? But now the LORD has abandoned us and left us in the power of the Midianites." Then the LORD turned to him and said, "Go in this strength of yours and save Israel yourself from the Midianites—am I not the one who is sending you?" But he said, "Please, sir, how should I be the one to save Israel? My clan is the poorest in Manasseh, and I am the least in my ancestral house." Then the LORD said to him, "But I will be with you, and you will defeat the Midianites to a man." He said to him, "If you will, sir, please give me some sign that it is You who are speaking with me. Do not leave here until I come back to you and take out my offering and set it down in front of you." And he said: "I will stay here until you return." Then Gideon went in and prepared a goat and unleavened bread from an *ephah* of flour; he put the meat in a basket and the broth in a pot and he took this out to him under the tree and presented it. Then the angel of God said to him: "Take the meat and the unleavened bread and set them on that rock, and spill out the broth." He did so. Then the angel of the LORD held out the staff that he had in his hand and touched the meat and the bread with its tip. A fire sprang up from the rock and engulfed the meat and the unleavened bread, and with that, the angel of the LORD disappeared from sight. When Gideon realized that it was indeed an angel of the LORD, he said, "Oh no! Oh LORD God—this means that I have seen the angel of the LORD face to face." And the LORD said to him, "It is all right, do not be afraid, you will not die." (Jdg. 6:11–23)

The angel who appears to Gideon starts out with an announcement that ought to have startled him: "The LORD is with you, you mighty warrior." It was not the first part of this sentence that was intended to be surprising: "The LORD is with you" was, apparently, just a pious way of saying "hello" in ancient Israel. (So at least it was understood by the author of the book of Ruth, who adopted it for that narrative; see Ruth 2:4.) But the rest of the angel's sentence, the "mighty warrior" part, certainly should have caught Gideon's attention, since at the moment he was hardly acting the part of a mighty warrior. How pathetic is this picture of a fellow so afraid of the raiding Midianites that he has to hide his spare grains of wheat inside a winepress! Was the stranger being sarcastic in coming up to the timorous Gideon and saying, "Hello, you mighty warrior!"? If so, Gideon does not notice; he is certainly unaware that this is "the angel of the LORD," or else he would do what everyone else does in such circumstances, bow down in reverential awe. Instead, he fixes on the stranger's pious greeting in order to give him a somewhat impious retort: "Oh yeah? If the LORD is with us, where is He now?" Then the angel turns to him and says, "Go in this strength of yours and save Israel yourself from the Midianites—am I not the one who is sending you?" Certainly this should have tipped him off: who could this "I" be if not God Himself? Yet it is only after the next exchange, when he is told, "But I will be with you, and you will defeat the Midianites to a man," that Gideon begins to suspect that the visitor is not an ordinary human. Even so, he is still not sure: he wants proof, a sign. This is the point of the prepared sacrifice. It is only after the flame magically consumes the offering and the angel himself disappears that Gideon's moment of confusion may truly be said to be over. The fog has at last lifted.

The Moment of Confusion

Here it might be appropriate to take a step backward and consider the whole phenomenon of the angelic messenger that we have been examining. Why should such an intermediary be necessary in the first place? After all, even the most primitive conception of God (or the gods, for that matter) holds that He can somehow affect human thought directly—sending dreams to some, for example, or speaking within their minds. So why should He bother sending these odd, humanlike figures that fool people for a while and then, at a certain point, come to be recognized for who they are?

The same question apparently bothered some Jews and Christians in the ancient world. One of them was the author of the Wisdom of Solomon, a book written just before the start of the common era, apparently by a Greek-speaking Jew who lived in Alexandria, Egypt.* By this time, the stories that we have been examining had been around for many centuries, and perhaps because he was acquainted with Greek philosophical ideas, he was disturbed by them. He did not like the idea of depicting God as actively intervening in the affairs of men, either by Himself or through some angel. Instead this author liked to think that it was an entity called *Wisdom* that actually did things on earth, while God remained in heaven. Now, Wisdom was a bit like the angels

---

* This book appears in some Christian Bibles as one of the biblical apocrypha, while others include it alongside Proverbs, Ecclesiastes, and other canonical works. It is not considered part of the Jewish Bible.

that we have been examining, a divine envoy of sorts, but an altogether spiritual one. Here, for example, is how this author describes the Israelites' exodus from Egypt:

> Wisdom delivered a holy people and blameless
> race from a nation of oppressors.
> She entered the soul of a servant of the Lord, and
> withstood dread kings with wonders and
> signs.
> She gave to holy people the reward of their labors;
> she guided them along a marvelous way, and
> became a shelter to them by day, and a starry
> flame through the night.
>
> (Wis. 10:15–17)

It is not difficult to discern this author's efforts to rationalize the miraculous events of the exodus. Here Wisdom enters the *soul* of a servant of the Lord (that is, Moses). This is presumably a reference to God's miraculous appearance to Moses in the burning bush (Exodus chapters 3–4). Significantly, however, she does not *appear* to Moses here, and there is no burning bush at all in this account; Wisdom simply enters Moses' soul. Then Wisdom stands up against the threats of Pharaoh by means of "wonders and signs." Certainly the ten plagues are the main feature of the exodus narrative in the Bible, an unequivocally miraculous series of events. They could hardly have been omitted, even by this author, but they are certainly being downplayed here: these signs and wonders simply become Wisdom's means of resisting a human tyrant. The pillar of cloud that guided the Israelites in the desert was, according to the Bible, an actual pillar seen by all; but here this pillar is converted into a figure of Wisdom's guidance of the people, providing them with (apparently metaphorical) shelter by day. The pillar of fire that guided the Israelites at night is similarly a "starry flame"—starry because this author would prefer to think that it was really the stars that lit the Israelites' way, rather than any actual, miraculous pillar as in the Exodus account. Throughout this passage—in fact, throughout the whole book—the very idea of Wisdom (a feminine noun in Greek: *sophia*) as God's intermediary is wonderfully ambiguous. On the one hand, it was possible to speak of "her" as having done this or that, but on the other, what is Wisdom if not some abstract, spiritual entity, or as this author elsewhere defines it, "the spirit of the Lord" that "fills the world," something "that holds all things together" (1:7)? It is not hard to see how the whole idea of Wisdom in this book functions as a bridge between two domains that are otherwise completely separate, the spiritual and the material. God's spirit may fill the world, but He Himself remains aloof, somewhere in heaven. Indeed, the things that happen in the material world may take place because of Wisdom's inspiration or underlying presence, but they are nevertheless material, while Wisdom herself is by nature invisible and intangible, that is, spiritual.

This is precisely what angels are not in the Bible. They look like men, they talk like men, they can sit down and walk around and maybe even eat like men. Then, all of sudden, the whole thing turns out to have been an illusion: their true identity is revealed, and people realize who they are and bow down in reverence.

How is the Wisdom of Solomon's way of conceiving things different from that seen above, in passages from the books of

Genesis, Joshua, and Judges? One might certainly say that the Wisdom of Solomon's view is more rationalistic, but let us leave such labels aside for the moment. Rather, I would prefer to say that the world in which angels can suddenly appear or disappear is a world in which the border between the spiritual and the physical is not all that clear, or at least not all that respected. What life seems to be can change in a minute to something else, and everyone in the biblical world is apparently ready for such a change to occur. As we have seen, the moment of recognition comes with some surprise, *but no incomprehension* on the part of human beings: they know, in other words, that the spiritual realm is always there, ready to intrude on the physical. What is more, the fog I have mentioned—whereby the most obvious hints of the angel's true identity pass unnoticed by the human beings—seems to imply that these intrusions of the spiritual can indeed be overlooked by the best of us, that the little indications that such an intrusion is occurring sometimes pass us by.

In the light of all this, the moment of confusion begins to come into somewhat clearer focus. It seems to straddle two realms: what we might call regular reality and the supernatural. The fact that people are confused for a while appears to be a necessary element, a way of indicating how these two realms overlap, or can overlap, without people noticing anything at first. Indeed, the moment of confusion always leads to that sudden *click* whereby an ordinary encounter turns out to be something else entirely. It is all about perception, something that suddenly opens in the human mind. The biblical figure's confusion announces this fact, indeed celebrates it, which is apparently why these biblical narratives seem to make so much of it.

The Moment of Confusion

ᘏ ᘏ ᘏ

Balaam is an ambiguous figure in the book of Numbers. Something of a seer or visionary, he is offered a large sum of money to curse Israel (since cursing was felt to be an effective means of harming someone in the biblical world). Balaam willingly takes the job. This certainly did not speak well of him—not only did he use his visionary gifts for personal gain, but he tried to turn them against an entirely innocent people. But then, instead of cursing Israel, Balaam ends up reversing himself, blessing Israel not once but several times. These blessings seemed to argue in favor of Balaam. After all, no matter what he intended at first, he did end up *helping* Israel with his words. What is more, the Bible stresses that God "put His word in Balaam's mouth." He thus seems to have been nothing less than a true prophet.

It is against this background that a peculiar incident with Balaam's donkey should be read, since it is clearly designed to portray this prophet for hire in an unambiguously negative light.

> He was riding on his donkey, with his two servant-boys alongside, when the donkey saw an angel of the LORD standing in the middle of the road with his sword drawn in his hand. The donkey went running off the road and into a field. Balaam hit the donkey to get it to go back on the road, but by then the angel of the LORD was standing in a pathway of the vineyards, with a fence on either side. When the donkey saw the angel of the LORD, it squeezed up against the wall, pressing Balaam's leg against it. He kept on hitting it. The angel of the LORD then moved around until he stood in a place so narrow that there

> was no room to turn to the right or left. When the donkey now saw the angel of the LORD, it just lay down underneath Balaam. This made Balaam furious, and he hit the donkey even harder with his stick. Then the LORD opened the donkey's mouth and it said to Balaam, "What have I done to you to make you hit me three times?" Balaam said to the donkey, "You've put me to shame! Why, if I had a sword in my hand, I would have killed you by now." Then the donkey said to Balaam, "Am I not your own donkey! Haven't you been riding on me from long ago to this very day? Have I ever acted this way in the past?" And he said: "No."
>
> Then the LORD opened Balaam's eyes and he saw the angel of the LORD standing on the road with his sword in his hand, so Balaam prostrated himself and bowed to the ground. (Num. 22:22–31)

"Some prophet!" the narrative seems to be saying. "At a crucial moment, even his donkey was more discerning than Balaam was."

This point aside, however, here we are once again confronted with a moment of confusion. The donkey suddenly shies from the middle of the road (as donkeys sometimes do; this hardly needed to be said in the ancient world), and Balaam does not understand why. In other words, here again is a narrative that presents an "angel of the LORD" appearing to someone (and again, as with Joshua, "with his sword drawn in his hand"), but the someone in question does not realize what is happening. Indeed, Balaam's lack of discernment is exceptional. It is not that he mistakes the angel for a human; rather he sees nothing at all. The donkey, who does see, does not merely remain immobile but actually tries to flee from the angel time and time again. Yet Balaam simply beats the donkey harder; this man must indeed be in some kind of fog. So thick is that fog that when the donkey actually starts speaking to him—but donkeys don't speak!—Balaam answers as if it were the most normal thing in the world. It is only when God opens Balaam's eyes that he at last discerns what was so obvious to the donkey and us readers—and then Balaam reacts just as every other human being does when his or her eyes are opened: he falls down to the ground in reverence.

The point of this narrative seems to be to put Balaam to shame. But this is accomplished by evoking elements that must have been familiar in the biblical world—the fog, the moment of confusion, the moment of recognition. In other words, this narrative too is telling a bit more than it seems to intend: it seeks to diminish Balaam's standing as a holy man, but it does so by tying into the conventions of a theme that we have seen before with Joshua, Manoah and his wife, Abraham and Sarah, and Gideon (none of them negative characters at all). The world in which such supernatural encounters occur seems like ordinary reality, or at least starts off that way. Then everything changes—putting not just people like Balaam to shame, but Manoah and his wife, Joshua, even Abraham. The most distinguished men and women of the spirit can be in a fog and fail to see the obvious.

ʚ ʚ ʚ

These moment-of-confusion narratives point us to a larger question: who exactly are the human-seeming angels that appear in them? An answer has been hinted at in some of the passages examined, but it is stated most clearly in Jacob's famous encounter with an angel at the crossing of the Jabbok River:

> And Jacob was left alone, and a man wrestled with him until the break of day. When he saw that he could not overcome him, he wrenched Jacob's hip in its socket, so that the socket of Jacob's hip was strained in the fight with him. Then he said, "Let go of me, since it is getting to be dawn." But Jacob said, "I will not let you go unless you bless me." He said, "What is your name?" and he answered, "Jacob." He said, "Your name will not be Jacob any longer, but Israel, since you have struggled with God and with men and have prevailed." Then Jacob said to him, "Please, now, tell me your name." He answered, "Why should you be asking for my name?" and he blessed him there. Jacob named the place Peniel, saying, "I have seen God face to face and yet my life has been spared." (Gen. 32:24–30)

There is little need to point out that Jacob's fight with the angel bears a strong resemblance to some of the narratives already examined. Thus, once again, the human being seems to be unaware of the angel's true identity: it is, from Jacob's point of view, "a man" with whom he wrestles all night. (However, that this "man" was indeed an angel was hardly in doubt even within the biblical period; apparently alluding to this same incident, the prophet Hosea says of Jacob, "In his strength he fought with God, he struggled with an angel and overcame him"—Hos. 12:3–4). It is difficult to know at what point Jacob finally grasps the truth. Perhaps he has already understood when he asks the mysterious stranger at dawn to bless him. If not, certainly he must know the truth when the stranger changes his name from Jacob to Israel and explains that "you have struggled with God." But once again, the moment of recognition seems to get relatively little attention. Indeed, Jacob then goes on to ask the same question that Manoah had asked *before* he was aware of his angel's true identity (and Jacob here gets the same answer that Manoah did, a polite "Mind your own business"). But all of this pertains to the preceding discussion.

One new, and particularly disturbing, element in this narrative is its assertion that Jacob has "struggled with God." The story, after all, says that he struggled with a man, and if Hosea and every subsequent reader of this story are right in saying that the man was really an angel, still, an angel is not God. The angel may have been sent by God, he may himself be a divine being, but he is nonetheless *not* God—in fact, that seems to be the very essence of being an angel: *not* being God. But if that is so, why does not this text say that Jacob's name was changed because he "struggled with an *angel* of God"? Why, in fact, does Jacob go on to name the place Peniel ("face of God") and offer as the reason the fact that "I have seen God face to face," when the narrative itself seems to be saying the opposite, that he has not seen God at all but a "man," that is, an angel or emissary of God?

I should note in passing how this struggle with God has been handled by translators and commentators throughout the ages. The Old Greek ("Septuagint") translation of the Hebrew Bible, going back to the third century B.C.E., translated, "For you *have been strong* with God, and you shall be powerful with men." One advantage of this translation was that it softened any idea of a direct, physical struggle with God (indeed, "with God" could even be understood as "with God's help"). Similarly, the ancient Aramaic translation of Onkelos reads: "For you *are great* before the LORD and among men; therefore you have prevailed." As for Jacob seeing God "face to face," Onkelos revises the text: "And Jacob called the name of the place Peniel, for 'I have seen *an angel of the* LORD face to face.' " The same tactics are employed by other ancient translators. Nor have modern translators been unaffected by these same issues. The New Revised Standard Version, a recent Protestant translation very popular in America, reads, "You have striven with God," but adds in a footnote: "Or *with divine and human beings*." The recent translation of the Jewish Publication Society translates: "For you have striven with *beings divine and human*," and goes on to say that Jacob named the place Peniel, meaning, "I have seen *a divine being* face to face."

৬ ৬ ৬

A modern biblical scholar might rightly point out that this narrative is designed to explain the origin of certain things—including the place-name Peniel (or in another form, Penuel) and the name of the nation made up of Jacob's descendants, Israel. Both of these name end in "el," and so in both cases the Bible seeks to explain the name by connecting it specifically with God (*El* or *Elohim* in Hebrew). Therefore, this argument runs, if the text says at the crucial point that Jacob struggled with *God* and saw *God* face-to-face, it does so only in order to account for the "el" in these names. Meanwhile, the supporting narrative makes it clear that he actually saw and fought with a man and not God himself (in keeping with the biblical preference to avoid face-to-face confrontations between God and humans).

Yet the Bible could have just as easily accounted for these "el" names by stating that Jacob had fought with an *angel of God*—certainly such an assertion would suffice to explain why both names end in this divine particle. Moreover, if the text sought ultimately to claim that, in fighting with an angel of God, Jacob was in effect fighting with God Himself, then why does the text not at least get us halfway there by saying outright in the story that Jacob's opponent was indeed an angel of God and not (as it actually says) simply a "man." Finally, if the difference between fighting with God and fighting with an angel is so obvious to translators, why did not this contradiction seem to bother ancient Israelites? It is right there in the book of Genesis; in fact, it did not seem to bother the prophet Hosea, either. His reflection on this incident, we should recall, was: "In his strength he fought *with God,* he struggled *with an angel* and overcame him." Hosea apparently saw no problem in referring to Jacob's opponent in the same breath as either God or an angel.

The real answer to this question has already been glimpsed in some of the passages cited earlier but needs now to be stated outright, however disquieting it may be. For as many scholars have noted, the distinction between God and angels does not seem to be consistently maintained, at least not in the oldest parts of the Bible. One almost has the impression that these biblical narratives attest to an awareness that the "angel" they speak of is really a construct, one might even say a literary device. What an "angel" really *is,* these texts are saying, is a way of reporting that God Himself appeared to someone in human form, or more precisely, in what *at first looked like human form.* After the angel has ascended on the flames of the altar, Manoah and his wife are worried: "We will surely die," they say, "because *we have seen God.*" "Go with these men," the angel says to Balaam, "but speak only what *I tell you* to speak" (Num. 22:35). These words may be spoken by the angel, but they are God's words: the "I" here refers to God and not some intermediary. (Note that God utters virtually the same sentence to Balaam, but without any intermediary, in a dream the night before—Num. 22:20.) Abraham sees three men, but then "the *LORD* said to Abraham, 'Why did Sarah laugh?'" The "angel of the LORD" appears to Gideon, but then "the *LORD* turned to him" and spoke. One might of course say that "God" or "LORD" in these instances really means "divine being." Alternately, one might say that these messengers represented their Master so perfectly and completely that they were altogether justified in using "I" when speaking on His behalf. One might even say that this was so not only when angels were delivering a prepared message, but also when they were reacting to something unexpected, such as Sarah's laughter. One might say any of these things. But the simple truth is that, for many of these biblical narratives, the "angel" never really ceases being God; the human form is a formality.

One last moment of confusion will make the point clear:

> Now Moses was tending the flocks of his father-in-law Jethro, the priest of Midian, and he led the flocks into the wilderness until he came to Horeb, the mountain of God. An angel of the LORD appeared to him in a blazing fire amidst a certain bush. And as he looked, behold! The bush was burning with fire, but the bush was not burned up. Then Moses said, "I must turn aside and see this great sight; why the bush is not burning up." When the LORD saw that he was turning aside to see, God called to him from out of the bush and said, "Moses, Moses." He said, "Here I am." He said, "Do not come any closer. Take your shoes from off your feet, for the place that you are standing on is holy ground." Then He said, "I am the God of your father, the God of Abraham, the God of Isaac, and the God of Jacob." Then Moses hid his face, because he was afraid to

> look at God. Then the LORD said, "I have seen the oppression of my people, who are in Egypt." (Ex. 3:1–7)

Moses is off grazing his father-in-law's sheep when he comes near to what the text calls "the mountain of God." Apparently it is God's wish to attract Moses' attention and bring him closer to the mountain—that is what the burning bush is all about, an unusual sight designed to get Moses to come closer. And Moses, like all the other figures examined thus far, does not really understand what is happening to him. Fascinated, he wonders: how can a bush keep burning and burning without burning up? So he approaches what he thinks is just a bush. The text had said that "an angel of the LORD appeared to him in a blazing fire amidst a certain bush," but the angel here is not said to have any human form—perhaps the bush itself serves as the "angel" here. In any case, from its midst comes a voice that turns out to be that of God (or "the LORD"), and soon, God/"the LORD" is conversing directly with Moses, as if the angel or the bush had ceased to stand between them. In other words, the angel is, once again, a mere formality. Indeed, what God says here is precisely what the "chief of the LORD's army" had said to Joshua in the passage with which we began, namely, "Take your shoes from off your feet, for the place that you are standing upon is holy ground." Now, of course, this is no coincidence; as scholars have noted, it seems as if Joshua is being pointedly portrayed in that passage in the same terms as are used of Moses here. But if so, one could hardly ask for a clearer demonstration that the human form (in this case, that of the "chief of the LORD's army") is a mere formality: the human form in one text turns out to be God in another.

Here, then, is the most important point about the angel in all of these texts. He is not so much an emissary, or messenger, of God as God Himself in human form. Now, I should stress again that this is not true of *all* angels in the Bible; moreover, to say "God in human form" has a certain built-in ambiguity, since such a being is, but also is not, God (that is, he is also this "human form," however illusory or fleeting that form may be). Nevertheless, reformulating the angel in these texts as really *God in human form* accounts for several things. It explains not only the easy transition from the angel identity to God Himself, but it also nuances further the issue with which we began, namely, the moment of confusion. This moment is required because the angel is essentially an illusion, a piece of the supernatural that poses as ordinary reality for a time. The angel, in other words, is not some lesser order of divine being; it is God Himself, but God unrecognized, God intruding into ordinary reality. The angel can thus be invisible, as the angel was to Balaam, or contained in a bush, as with Moses, but mostly he appears to be a fairly ordinary-looking human. Indeed, there does not seem to be any functional difference between an angel looking human or being invisible or contained in a bush, since, once the moment of confusion is over, this first, apparent reality will in any case dissolve into a wholly new reality, the reality of God's very being. So there must always be a moment of confusion, followed by a *click*. By the same token, this explains why, in the case of Abraham and of Jacob, the angels are not even called angels but men. If an angel were an actual, stable sort of creature, a real *messenger* of God, then every angel would no doubt be called an angel consistently. But he is not. His humanlike appearance is just a shill—he is actually God. So call him a man, call him an angel; it really does not matter, since this is only a temporary, and altogether illusory, state of being. For the same reason, these angels do not have names (there are no named angels until the very end of the biblical period). That is to say, the real answer to the question "What is your name?" asked of their angels by Jacob and Manoah is not the answer that they received ("Why should you ask my name?") but the same answer that Moses gets when, in the continuation of the passage cited above, he asks his interlocutor at the burning bush what *his* name is: "Thus shall you [Moses] say to the Israelites, "The LORD, the God of your fathers, the God of Abraham, the God of Isaac, and the God of Jacob has sent Me to you. This is My name forever, by this shall I be known for all eternity" (Ex. 3:15). The angel looks like an ordinary human being for a while, but only for a while; then comes the moment of recognition, when it turns out that, oh yes, that was God and no ordinary human.

⁂

What does this have to do with the Project?

There is, I think, an important difference between the way that most people nowadays (indeed, starting as early as the author of the Wisdom of Solomon) are accustomed to conceive of the spiritual and the way this same thing was conceived in ancient Israel, at least in the texts that we have been examining. There are not two realms in the Bible, this world and the other, the spiritual and the material—or rather, these two realms are not neatly segregated but intersect constantly. God turns up around the street corner, dressed like an ordinary person. He does not "enter the soul of a righteous man," He appears in an actual brushfire at the foot of a mountain. And it is not even that, on such occasions, He enters the world as we conceive of it from somewhere else. Rather, it seems that the world itself as we conceive of it (at least the biblical world) has little cracks in it here and there. We conceive of it in one way, and most of the time it goes along with that conception; but now and again people turn out not to be people and ordinary reality turns out to be something quite different from what we thought. That is the whole point of the *fog*—donkeys start talking, perfect strangers seem somehow to know your wife's name, fires burn on and on, and so forth.

These biblical texts could, of course, have been written differently. They could have angels who truly are messengers of God and do not, as we have seen, fade into God Himself; and these messengers could announce things, or do things, in a straightforward fashion to people who are not in a fog. The moment of confusion need have had no role in these narratives. The fact that it does, in text after text (even if, after a time, it became conventional), suggests that there was something essential about this confusion. It represents the biblical authors' most realistic sense of the way things actually are. The spiritual is not something tidy and distinct, another order of being. Instead, it is perfectly capable of intruding into everyday reality, as if part of this world. It is not just "in here"; it is also out there, a presence, looming.

3

Not Searching for God

> Now Terah took his son Abram, and his grandson Lot (Haran's son), and Abram's wife Sarai (his daughter-in-law), and he set out with them from Ur of the Chaldeans for the land of Canaan; but when they got as far as Haran they stopped there. Terah lived to the age of 205; and Terah died in Haran. Then the LORD said to Abram, "Depart from your homeland, your clan and your father's house [that is, your immediate family], and go to the land I will show you. And I will make you into a great nation and bless you I will make your name great, so that it will become a blessing. I will bless those who bless you, and curse anyone who curses you, and all the families of the region will bless themselves by you." So Abram went forth as the LORD had commanded. (Gen. 11:31–12:4)

Above are the first words spoken by God to Abraham, the beginning of his lifelong encounter with this deity. What God says to Abraham is, from a formal standpoint, rather unexceptional:

"Do what I tell you to do and it will go well with you." The promised blessings are perhaps unusually emphatic, but they reflect later reality; from biblical times to the present day, Abram/Abraham has been revered as the ancestor of millions—his name has indisputably "become a blessing."* One interesting feature of this passage for ancient interpreters was the extraordinary obedience that Abraham exhibits in it. Here God addresses Abraham for the very first time and does not even say where He wants Abraham to go other than "to the land I will show you," yet Abraham sets out without hesitation.

But none of these features is the reason for my citing these verses. Rather, what seems to me worth considering here (precisely because it is so rarely considered, in this or in a great many other passages in the Hebrew Bible) is what Abraham does to bring about this encounter with God: absolutely nothing. He does not pray, he does not fast, he indulges in no acts of self-mortification such as those practiced by mystics and seekers in later times. Nor does he have any past history of meritorious deeds that would make it logical or natural for God to turn to him. Presumably, Abraham is just walking along one day or sitting somewhere when God starts talking to him—but even to put things that way is to distort somewhat the character of this passage. What Abraham was doing or had done before was just not

---

* Translators often misrepresent this text as saying that Abraham himself will "become a blessing." Actually, the text means that Abraham's *name* will become a blessing, in the most concrete sense—that is, his name will be used in blessing other people: "May you be like Abraham" (for a parallel, see Gen. 48:20).

important from the text's standpoint: God spoke to Abraham and that was all that mattered.

I have chosen this passage among many possible candidates that make my point because, in the case of this passage, we are fortunate to have a rewording of it by a somewhat later anonymous writer, the author of the *Book of Jubilees*. We do not know the precise date of this book's composition, but in my opinion (and that of many others) it must have been written at or near the beginning of the second century B.C.E., which is to say, toward the end of the period of the Hebrew Bible but still more than two centuries before the start of Christianity. Its author was a Jew who probably lived in or near Jerusalem.

The *Book of Jubilees* is actually a commentary on the book of Genesis, but a commentary in the form of a rewriting (which was the most common form of biblical commentary in that period). That is, the author seeks to fill in the blanks in the book of Genesis by retelling the biblical story with all kinds of new details thrown in, details that answer commonly asked questions about the text. Such retellings also frequently revise what the original text had said in order to make it conform to ideas, assumptions, or ideological positions common in the reteller's own day. Here, then, is how this anonymous author rewrites the passage from Genesis cited above:

> And as he [Abraham] was sitting alone and making [astronomical] observations, something came into his heart, saying, "All the signs of the stars and the signs of the sun and the moon are in the hand of the LORD. Why am I searching? If He wishes, He will make it rain morning and evening, and if He wishes He will not send [rain] down. Everything is in His

hand." And he prayed that night, saying, "My God, the Most High God, You alone are God to me. You created everything, and everything that is was made by Your hands, and You and Your kingdom I have chosen. Save me from the evil spirits that rule over the thoughts of a man's heart, and do not let them lead me away from following You, O my God. Establish me and my seed forever, and let us not go astray henceforth forever." Then he said, "Shall I return to Ur of the Chaldeans, who are entreating me to return to them, or should I remain in this place? Make your servant choose the right path so that he may fulfill [it] and so that I not walk in any deceitfulness of my own mind, O my God." And when he finished speaking and praying [thus], the word of the LORD was sent to him by [an angel], saying: "Depart from your homeland, your clan and your father's house, and go to the land I will show you. And I will make you into a great nation . . . [etc., as in Gen. 12:1]." (*Jubilees* 12:17–22)

There are, of course, many interesting aspects to this rewriting, but what is striking for the present discussion is that God's words to Abraham no longer come unbidden. Abraham actually initiates the process by praying to God, and God's first words to him, "Depart from your homeland," are thus, according to the *Book of Jubilees,* an answer to a human being's prayer. This does not appear to be an incidental detail. Apparently, it seemed more appropriate to the author of *Jubilees* that God should respond to a prayer by Abraham than suddenly start speaking to him without warning or prior invitation, as the Bible relates.

A retelling of God's first words to Abraham occurs in another text from the same period, the *Apocalypse of Abraham.* It is very different from the retelling in *Jubilees,* but there is one element that the two texts share. Here Abraham, speaking in the first person, recounts how he became exasperated at his father's worship of idols. Convinced that there is only one true God, Abraham says to him:

> "Listen, Terah my father, I will examine with you the question of who is the God who created all these gods whom we take care of [in a pagan temple]. For, who is He, or what is He, that made the sky blue? Who made the sun golden, who put light into the moon and the stars along with it? Who is He who has made the dry land amidst the oceans, and has given you the power of speech? Let God Himself appear to us!" And as I was thus talking to my father Terah in the courtyard of my house, the voice of the Almighty came down from heaven in a flood of fire, exclaiming, "Abraham, Abraham!" And I said, "Here I am." And the voice said, "You are seeking God the Creator by the understanding of your mind. It is I. Leave your father, Terah, and leave his house, so that you as well do not perish in the sins of your father's house."

The last sentence, it should be clear, is a free reworking of Gen. 12:1, "Depart from your homeland, your clan and your father's house." It is noteworthy, then, that once again this sentence is not uttered by God unprompted, as in Genesis, but comes in response to a request by Abraham, "Let God Himself appear to us!" Indeed, Abraham is described here as "*seeking* God the Creator" before He actually appears to him. Once again, the later writer has "improved" the book of Genesis, which says not a word about Abraham seeking God or asking Him to reveal Himself—nor, of course, anything about Abraham's virtuous denunciation of worshiping idols.

This is not an isolated phenomenon; it appears in other writings that have survived from the same period as that of *Jubilees* and the *Apocalypse of Abraham*. For example, the *Testament of Levi*, a text going back to the first or second century B.C.E., has its putative author, Jacob's son Levi, recount that a "spirit of understanding from the LORD" came over him:

> "And I observed all men having gone astray. Unrighteousness had built itself walls and injustice was enshrined in towers. I kept grieving over the race of men, and I prayed to the LORD that I might be saved. Then sleep fell upon me and I beheld a high mountain. . . . And behold, the heavens were opened and an angel of the LORD spoke to me."

Here, there is no biblical original to which to compare this text, but it is striking nonetheless that it is the human being who initiates the divine-human encounter, and again, as with Abraham in the two previous examples, by means of a prayer. Now, God here actually has something he wants to tell Levi. As the angel goes on to explain, God has designated a special role for him and his descendants. "He will separate you from injustice and make you his son and servant and a minister of His presence" (an allusion to Levi's special role as the ancestor of the priestly tribe, the one that will act as God's servants and ministers in the Jerusalem temple). Nonetheless God does not, as it were, open the conversation but addresses Levi only in response to his prayer (and even then only in a dream, and only via an intermediary angel, as in *Jubilees*).

The same is true of Ezra in the (slightly later) *Apocalypse of Esdras:*

> [Ezra says:] It came to pass in the thirty-second year and on the twentieth day of the month that I was in my house. And I cried out, saying to the LORD Most High, "LORD, grant me the privilege to see the mysteries." And when it was night there came an angel, Michael the archangel, and he said to me: "Starting tomorrow, Ezra, you must abstain [from food] for seventy days." And I fasted as he told me. And the angel Raphael came and gave me a stick of incense. And I fasted for two times five weeks [seventy days], and then I saw God's mysteries and his angels." (*Apocalypse of Esdras* 1:1–5)

Once again, the divine revelation does not just occur but comes in response to a human prayer. Indeed, here Ezra embarks on a course of self-abnegation that was to become familiar in later times: he fasts in order to bring about the induction into the "mysteries" that he has requested. Only then does God, or rather, God's angelic emissary, appear to him. The same is true of the Syriac *Apocalypse of Baruch* from this same period. There, God instructs Baruch to

> purify yourself for seven days: eat no bread, drink no water, and speak to no one. And afterwards, come to this place and I will reveal Myself to you and tell you hidden truths, and give you instruction about the course of the times, for they are coming, and there will be no delay. (2 *Baruch* 20:5–6)

The evidence from the late biblical period is not altogether one-sided, of course. There still are texts in which God sometimes appears unbidden. Nevertheless, there is no doubt that a change has occurred. In much of the literature of this later period, God must be sought after, approached with prayer or fasting, and only by someone of demonstrated (or invented) virtue. As we saw in the case of Abraham, even a well-known biblical passage like Gen. 12:1–3 was rewritten to conform to the new pattern.

In much of the Hebrew Bible, by contrast, God simply buttonholes people and starts speaking. He appears unbidden to Jacob at Bethel. Jacob has done nothing in particular to bring about this dream vision and is in fact frightened by it; if it were up to him, he would presumably have chosen to do without it. Nor does Jacob have a particularly glorious past that would have led God to start speaking with him. (All we know of his past is that he at one point cheated his brother out of his birthright and, somewhat later, tricked his poor, blind father into giving him a blessing meant for someone else—not a very distinguished record.) God contrives to bring Moses to the burning bush and starts speaking to him there—again, Moses did nothing on his own to initiate this encounter and, judging by his initial reaction, most likely would have preferred that it not occur. There may be an exception or two to this general pattern (Balaam seems repeatedly to invite God's word—and even pay for it by setting up an altar with rich sacrifices; Solomon massively sacrifices to God at Gibeah and is rewarded with a dream vision), but they are exceptions that prove the rule.

It is certainly relevant that in all these cases, writers at the time of *Jubilees* and the other texts seen also sought to make over the figures in question so as to justify God's choice of them. As noted, until the day that God addressed him in Gen. 12:1, Abraham had no history of good deeds or meritorious action in his past. But *Jubilees,* in common with other books from the same period, insists that he did: Abraham was no less than the discoverer of monotheism, the one to figure out that all other gods were false and that there was only one divine power in the universe. *That,* according to these sources, is why God chose Abraham and promised him all those blessings. But of course there is not a word about such things in Genesis itself. Jacob was similarly retrofitted with righteousness: he became, in *Jubilees,* a pious scholar and dutiful son, ultimately the favorite of the same blind father he had cheated—but again, there is nothing of this in Genesis. Moses and other heroes were given similarly appropriate, pious biographies by the same ancient writers, and presumably all for the same reason: it did not seem proper to them that God should choose just anyone, appearing out of nowhere to start speaking to someone who neither had a distinguished past nor had prayed earnestly for God to appear. But that seems to be precisely what these biblical narratives themselves maintain.

All this is interesting, it seems to me, precisely because our age is one in which God is axiomatically remote, a time of "the eclipse of God." He does not just start talking to people, at least not to most people deemed sane by the relevant authorities. We are much closer to the way of thinking evidenced in works like *Jubilees* and the *Testament of Levi* in believing that God speaks, or has spoken, only with the exceptionally righteous and only after having been sought out. Of course, we ourselves may pray to God and hope for an answer, but in this we are at best in the same boat as the biblical heroes in *Jubilees* and similar books—indeed, worse off, since our prayers do not necessarily merit the same direct and immediate response that they got. So what has happened? Is it simply the case that God ceased to speak unbidden to human beings sometime in the middle of the biblical period?

ɞ ɞ ɞ

One feature of the Bible that has long been recognized by scholars is the *prophetic call narrative*. Time and time again the Bible tells us how this or that person first became a prophet, and the circumstances have an astonishing regularity about them. The prophet in question never seeks out God; it is always the opposite—and God's initiative is usually met with some reluctance, if not outright refusal, by the prophet in question. Thus Moses:

> But Moses said to God, "Who am *I* that I should go to Pharaoh and lead the Israelites out of Egypt?" And He said, "I will be with you. . . ." But Moses said to the LORD, "Please, my Lord, I am no man of words, nor was I yesterday or the day before, nor from the time that You started speaking with Your servant. No, I am a slow and poor speaker." And the LORD said to him, "Who gives peoples mouths to speak, or who makes them dumb, or deaf, or seeing, or blind? Is it not I, the LORD? Now go! I will be with you and with your mouth, and I will teach you whatever you are to say." But Moses said, "Please, my Lord. Send someone else of Your choosing." (Ex. 3:11, 4:10–13)

And Isaiah:

> In the year that King Uzziah died, I saw my Lord seated high up on a lofty throne, whose skirts filled the temple. . . . And

> I said, "Woe is me! I am as good as dead. For I have impure lips, and I live among a people of impure lips—yet my eyes behold the King, the LORD of Hosts." But then one of the seraphim flew toward me carrying a coal, which he had picked up with tongs from off the altar, and he touched it to my mouth and said, "Now that this has touched your lips, your sin is gone and your wrongdoing has been done away with." Then I heard the LORD's voice saying, "Who can I send? Who will go for us?" And I said, "I am here. Send me." (Isa. 6:1, 5–8)

And Jeremiah:

> The word of the LORD came to me, saying: "Before I even shaped you in the womb, I knew you. And before you were born, I had consecrated you. I made you a prophet for the nations." But I said, "Oh no! O LORD God, I do not know how to speak—I am only a youth." But the LORD said to me, "Do not say, 'I am only a youth.' Wherever I send you, you will go, and whatever I tell you to say, you will say. Do not be afraid of them, for I will be with you to save you, says the LORD." (Jer. 1:4–8)

Why should the Bible bother to tell us how it was that X or Y became a prophet—and that he was at first unwilling to take on the job? One function that scholars have identified in such passages is that of legitimation. It is not that Moses or Samuel (see 1 Samuel 3) or Isaiah or Jeremiah was a self-promoter, these texts seem to say. On the contrary, when God called to him for the first time, the future prophet tried to refuse, or (in the case of Samuel) he was so little expecting a call from God that he mistook the divine voice for a human one.

Such may indeed be one reason why these passages exist, but this hardly accounts for everything. Why, for example, did not Samuel or Isaiah or Jeremiah actually try to turn the job down (as Moses did) if that was the whole point? Isaiah's reaction is *fear,* fear that he will die for having seen God; once purified and reassured on that score, he even volunteers for his prophetic role. Jeremiah's objection—I am too young—is set aside with an assurance that is anything but reassuring: "I will be with you to save you" (presumably from your many future opponents). Is Jeremiah's acceptance of such reassurance truly the reaction of one who shuns the prophet's calling? I do not wish to go too far; certainly the prophet's reluctance is a real element to be considered; indeed, it seems to have become a somewhat conventional feature in later times. But it seems more to the point to say that the way in which God simply summons prophets—rather than responding to something they did beforehand, as God responds to Abraham's prayer and meritorious past in *Jubilees* or to Levi's virtuous prayer in the *Testament of Levi*—is telling us something basic about reality as it was perceived earlier in the biblical period. Such things just happen, these texts seem to be saying, and to anyone.

The "to anyone" needs to be fleshed out a bit, since this also corresponds to another feature of the Bible well known to modern scholars. Biblical narratives often seem to delight in, or at least not hide from, the wholly inappropriate character of God's chosen servants. In the book of Judges, for example, God chooses (as we have already seen) Gideon, who points out that he is from "the weakest clan in Manasseh, and I am the youngest in my father's house" (Jdg. 6:15). God's other improbable choices in that book include the illegitimate son of a prostitute who supports himself as a highwayman (Jephthah); an impulsively violent man who marries a daughter of the enemy Philistines for a time, consorts with prostitutes, and ultimately surrenders to the sexual blackmail of Delilah (Samson); and a woman—not usually the stuff of leadership in ancient Israel, but in this case she actually goes on to lead a four-star general into battle (Deborah). Jesse shows all the logical candidates for king to the prophet Samuel (1 Samuel 16); Eliab, the oldest, seems to the prophet the one best suited for the job, but God rejects him out of hand. Ultimately, the divine choice falls on the one son so unlikely that Jesse had not even bothered to call him in from the fields (David). Saul, David's predecessor, had seemed so far from the normal divine servant that, when he fell in with a band of prophets, people said in astonishment, "Is Saul also among the prophets?" (1 Sam. 10:11). (Translation: What's someone like *him* doing with people like *them*?)

Of course, historiography, even by modern standards, has some constraints imposed on it. I am not suggesting that the facts or traditions should have been arbitrarily changed or a new past invented out of whole cloth. But there are many ways to talk about past events. That biblical authors show no hesitation in reporting on the rather dubious character or qualifications of these divinely chosen figures seems to be an important finding. Biblical narratives actually seem to highlight the fact that their heroes are far from the logical choice and, sometimes, far from pious or meritorious: these men and women have done nothing to deserve this sudden change in their status and they have certainly not sought it out on their own. Rather, it seems that they have been chosen for reasons that are inscrutable, or perhaps for no reason at all, and in this fact the biblical narratives seem to take some pleasure.

In a famous passage, the book of Amos describes a prophet's calling in these terms: "If a lion roars, who will not be frightened? If my LORD God has spoken, who will not be a prophet?" (Amos 3:8). In other words, prophesying is a natural response to the divine stimulus: it can happen to anyone. This was apt not only in summing up Amos's own particular path to prophecy (before God spoke to him, he had been a sheep rancher); it applies to nearly all the figures that we have been surveying. Their hearing God's voice, and acting in response to it, is presented as having occurred (to use an apt expression) out of the blue. They did little or nothing to deserve it and nothing to initiate it. Interestingly, though, these prophets and other chosen servants are surprised *but not astonished*. Like the various figures seen in Chapter 2, that God should come a-calling does not leave them utterly flabbergasted. Indeed, the future prophets not only know how to react, they even have enough self-possession to argue with God, mentioning problems that might hinder them or proposing that He choose someone else instead. In other words, the texts seem to start from the assumption that such encounters do take place, that God approaches human beings quite unbidden, and that when He does, a person will know (or eventually figure out) with whom he is speaking and how to respond.

ɞ ɞ ɞ

All this stands in sharp contrast to the writings of later times. People have to seek God out. This might seem counterintuitive, since later thinkers also insisted (as our earliest biblical texts do not) that God is everywhere, omnipresent and omniscient. If so, why is He so hard to find? Nevertheless, these same later sources maintain, human beings are always "in search of God." The paradox was not lost on the medieval Hebrew poet Yehudah ha-Levi, who asked: "Where can I find You? And where can I not find You?"

The search for God thus became the central theme of much later piety. The great medieval philosopher Maimonides declared the knowledge of God (which for him was not merely an *amor Dei intellectualis* but a living encounter) to be the goal and the highest good to which a human being might attain. Long before him, poets and sages described the search for God—it was a standard motif of medieval Hebrew poetry. Here, for example, is a lovely little poem written in Hebrew by Solomon ibn Gabirol in Spain in the eleventh century:

> Morning and eve have I searched for You and,
> looking upward, held up my hands.
> To you do I cry, with heart athirst—I'm like a
> pauper begging at my doorstep.
> The heights of heaven cannot contain You—yet
> You find a place amidst my thoughts.
> I try to hide your name in my heart, yet desire for
> You overcomes me, till it passes my lips.
> So I will praise the name of the Lord—as long as
> the breath of the living God is in my nostrils.

As usual, this medieval Hebrew poem is full of biblical allusions—but one must be careful! Many biblical texts say things like, "I have searched for You," and, "I have been zealous for

You," but in biblical Hebrew these expressions really mean "I have beseeched You [for something]," "I have earnestly sought Your favor." Not so in medieval poetry. What ibn Gabirol means in his first line is that—like everyone else—he is searching *for* God, praying "with heart athirst." What he wants in this poem (it is, of course, an altogether stylized request, meant to be spoken on behalf of the whole congregation) is not what people want in biblical prayers—help, and the sooner the better!—but *contact;* he has been searching "morning and eve" (that is, in the daily, fixed prayers of Judaism). But this is obviously not something easily attained: that is why he feels like a pauper entreating passersby for a handout. Then comes the key line: "The heights of heaven cannot contain You—yet You find a place amidst my thoughts." God is not encompassed by any physical locale, but He exists somehow, nonetheless, in the poet's mind. In fact, the poet says that God's name is so great within him that it has to find expression, to come out—and so it does, in this song, and in the liturgical praise that it is intended to introduce. A beautiful thought—but how far we are from the world of Abraham and Amos!

It is interesting how later tradition takes account of this apparent gap between the way things were in biblical times and the way things were later on (and are now). One well-known motif has it that *prophecy ceased* shortly after the period of the Babylonian exile (sixth century B.C.E.). For while the Bible contains the writings of a few prophets acknowledged to have lived shortly after the return from Babylonian exile, the centuries that followed had no canonical prophets: "When the later prophets died—Haggai, Zechariah, and Malachi—the capacity for prophecy departed from Israel" (b. Talmud, *Yoma* 9b). (As usual, historians know that the facts are somewhat more complicated. There is plenty of evidence of prophets and would-be prophets who circulated long after the return from exile, indeed, well past the start of the common era. Perhaps it would be more correct to say that prophecy fell into doubt, while some of its former functions were taken over by nonprophetic figures, sages and biblical interpreters.)

When people now turned to God for help, they sometimes evoked the absence of prophets and other worthy intercessors as the reason for God's apparent remoteness, or after the Jerusalem temple was again destroyed, its absence was evoked as the reason. In any case, things were obviously different now—of this there was no doubt—and the change was attributed to these differences in Israel's external circumstances. This idea gave birth to a new genre of supplication, a kind of Hebraic *"Ubi sunt?"*

> Gone are the men of faith, who came in the
> strength of their deeds!
> Mighty ones who stood in the breach, turning
> back God's decrees—
> They were our bulwark, and a shelter from God's
> wrath.
> Appeasing with whispered prayers, they turned
> back any anger against us.
> Even before they cried out, You would answer—
> for they knew how to entreat.
> Because of them You showed fatherly mercy; You
> never turned them down.
> But we have lost them for our sins; for our
> wrongdoing they are no longer.

The God of Old

They have gone to eternal rest, leaving us to our
sorrows.

('Anshei 'Amanah)

Lord, where are those acts of kindness—told to us
by our fathers—
That You once did for us?
So long as Your presence stood in the Tabernacle
readied for You—
There You would speak to us.
But now You have departed, oh, where is Your
glorious presence,
Which is no longer with us?

('Ayyeh Ḥasadekha)

Has the remnant of Zion's stock forgotten how to
entreat?
Or does God in His wrath withhold mercy?
He has left His Temple and footstool, neglected it
in His anger—
He would not so do in His mercy.
Where are His wonders, the deeds our fathers
recounted,
That He granted in His mercy?

(She'erit Peleṭat 'Ariel)

Thus began the search for God. Or did it? A glance at the book of Psalms might make one think otherwise. After all, isn't the psalmist constantly searching for God? "Shine forth, O You who are enthroned on the cherubim" (Ps. 80:1). But a closer look will reveal that this is not really so. The search spoken of in the book of Psalms is never for God's presence per se, but for His *help*. He may be asked to "shine forth" and make Himself known. He may sometimes even be described as far off from the *speaker* (that is, God is neglecting him), but He Himself is not unreachable. For the most part He is right there, in fact—but His attention needs to be aroused.

> Arise, why do You sleep, O LORD? Awake, do not
> neglect us for forever.
> Why should You hide Your face and forget our
> being oppressed?
> We are sunk down in the dirt, crawling facedown
> on the ground.
> Rise up and help us, redeem us in keeping with
> Your kindness.
>
> (Ps. 44:23–26)

> O LORD, my foes are so numerous! Many are
> those who attack me.
> Many say of me, "There is no deliverance for him
> through God." . . .
> Rise up, O LORD! Save me, O my God!
>
> (Ps. 3:1–2, 7)

> O LORD, do not withdraw Your mercy from me;
> let Your kindness and faithfulness always
> protect me.

> For innumerable misfortunes have swept over me;
> my sins have caught up with me, so that now
> I cannot see;
> I have more woes than the hairs of my head; I am
> losing my mind.
> O LORD, be kind and rescue me; O LORD, hurry
> to my aid.
>
> (Ps. 40:11–13)

In the book of Psalms God is often said to "hide His face," that is, withhold His favor. It is this situation of divine neglect that so many psalms seem designed to redress. The psalmist's oft-repeated question is not "How can I know You?" nor yet "How can I reach You?" but rather "How long is this going to take?" As with the cry of the victim (see Chapter 5), it is simply a matter of attracting God's attention and stirring up His feelings. That is why so many biblical texts describe various figures as making themselves piteous and miserable: David grovels like a dog (2 Sam 12:16), Ahab fasts and puts on sackcloth and ashes (1 Kings 21:27), Esther and Mordecai fast (Esth. 4:1–3), and so forth. It is also why in so many psalms the speaker goes on at great length about his own lowly state, frequently identifying himself as poor, downtrodden, or oppressed. Apparently, it is only necessary to arouse God's natural pity:

> My wounds stink and fester because of my own
> foolishness.
> I am all bent and bowed down; I walk around in
> gloom.
> My sinews are full of fever, nothing in my body is
> right.

Not Searching for God

I am completely crushed down, I cry out from the pains inside me.
O LORD, You know what I am asking; my groans do not escape You.
My mind reels, my strength has left me; even my eyes have lost their power.
My friends and companions stand aghast at what has befallen me; my family keeps its distance. . . .
Do not abandon me, LORD; my God, do not be far from me.
Hurry to my aid, O LORD my salvation.
(Ps. 38:5–11, 21–22)

Have mercy on me, LORD, for I am in distress.
My eyes are wasted by vexation, my mind along with my body.
My life is spent in pain, my years end with a sigh.
My strength is failing because of my sins, my limbs are wasting away.
I am put to shame by all my enemies, by my neighbors exceedingly;
I am a horror to my acquaintances; those who see me in the street avoid me.
Like a dead man, I am forgotten; I am like a possession given up for lost.
I have heard how they speak ill of me, intrigue on all sides,
As they scheme together against me, plotting to take my life.

But I have put my trust in You, LORD; I have declared You to be my God.
My fate is in Your hands. Save me from my enemies and pursuers.

(Ps. 31:9–15)

Have mercy on me, O LORD, for I am downtrodden;
Heal me, O LORD, for my bones shake with fear.
I am so afraid, while You, LORD—O, how long?
O LORD, return! Rescue me! Save me as befits Your faithfulness.

(Ps. 6:2–4)

How long, O LORD, will you keep ignoring me?
How long will You hide Your face from me?
How long will I have cares on my mind, grief in my heart all day long?
How long will my enemy lord it over me?
Look and answer me, O LORD, my God!
Restore the power to my eyes, lest I sleep the sleep of death—
Lest my enemy say, "I have gotten him," lest my foes exult at my fall.
But I trust in your faithfulness, my heart will exult in Your deliverance.

(Ps. 13:1–5)

So common is this phenomenon in the book of Psalms that an earlier generation of biblical scholars actually maintained that the psalms were composed to serve as a kind of "poor man's offering"—that is, they must have been meant to be recited by indigent Israelites who were unable to afford animal sacrifices to God, since in so many the speaker is described as poor and miserable. Nowadays, most scholars recognize that this view is misguided. Even kings, when they approach God in the Bible, are said to be downtrodden and oppressed, since that is the condition most likely to bring a response from God. It is God's nature to be merciful and loving, if only the facts of the case can be brought before Him—and so the psalmist weeps or calls out "in a loud voice." In the Hebrew Bible, God does not so much administer justice as He feels pity for the poor humans; He administers mercy.

૯ ૯ ૯

If so, why did things ever change?

One hypothesis suggests itself to explain the gap between God's closeness as reflected in much of the Hebrew Bible and His apparent remoteness later on, when He must be searched for. In ancient Israel, as we have seen, God was deemed to be present in His temple(s)—that is what an ancient Near Eastern temple was, a "house" in which the god was deemed to reside. But God's house was ultimately destroyed by the Roman army in the year 68 of the common era. Thereafter there was no physical structure in which He was thought to dwell. Is this not why He had to be searched for by later generations?

This explanation is, on the face of it, wrong or at least incomplete, since many of the later texts we have been examining—texts like *Jubilees* or the *Testament of Levi*—were nonetheless written long before the Roman army's invasion, when the

Jerusalem temple was still the central religious reality in the minds of all Jews (even if some felt it was in need of reform). But the matter of God's house is nonetheless worth pausing over. There had always been certain places on the Israelite landscape that were specifically associated with the presence of God. These included not only the sites of various temples, such as Shiloh and Bethel and Jerusalem, but other locations to which holiness was attached. Indeed, though it was not remarked upon at the time, a number of the passages examined in Chapter 2 specifically mention the site at which God's angel appeared, presumably because it was, or was to become, a well-known sacred locale. God thus appears to Moses at Horeb, "the mountain of God"; to Abraham at the "oak trees of Mamre"; to Gideon "beneath the oak tree in Ophrah"; to Jacob at Bethel, and so forth. True, in other narratives—such as that of Joshua near Jericho, or in the incidents involving Manoah and his wife or Balaam and his donkey—the place mentioned does not appear to have had any particular association with God in Israelite tradition; indeed, the last two narratives do not specify any place at all. Nevertheless, the fact that God is connected with, or held to frequent, certain spots is hardly irrelevant to our discussion.

Long ago, students of comparative religion highlighted the role of *sacred place* in the religious imagination of peoples around the world. Space, to a certain way of thinking, is not the homogenous and smooth continuum of modern thought, but is constantly broken up and made discontinuous by spots of holiness. Such are the sites of temples in many ancient civilizations, including those mentioned above. But rather than see God's proximity as a *result* of the existence of such sacred sites, it would seem more reasonable to suppose that the opposite is true. That is, it is precisely because God is so potentially present that He can crop up here or there on earth, indeed, here *and* there, since His being present at one sacred spot does not necessarily eliminate his being in another. To be sure, there is an element of mutuality here: an ancient Israelite who *knows* that God is in residence just over there, on that hill or in that temple, can scarcely need to search for God in the manner of later seekers. But at the same time, the very fact that this ancient Israelite can conceive of God in such a fashion, as residing in a particular spot, seems to reflect a profoundly different way of thinking about God from that attested in later times. *That* God is indeed close by, appearing unbidden to future prophets, revealing Himself to various people in a way that at first makes Him seem like an ordinary human. It is this whole way of conceiving of God that makes it possible for Him to inhabit a particular spot at all.

ɞ ɞ ɞ

What seems more to the point in our discussion is a change observed long ago by biblical scholars. As the biblical period goes on, God becomes bigger and more remote. The same God who buttonholes the patriarchs and speaks to Moses face-to-face is perceived in later times as a huge, cosmic deity—not necessarily invisible or lacking a body, but so huge as to surpass our own capacities of apprehension, almost our imagination:

> Who has measured the oceans in the hollow of his hand [as God has], or marked off the skies with a yardstick?

> Or put the earth's soil in his bushel, weighed the mountains on a hand-scale and the hills in a balance? . . .
> The nations themselves are a drop from the bucket [to Him], they weigh as much as dust on a scale.
> The islands He can flick off like a mote; all the Lebanon will not supply His kindling, its animals do not equal one lone offering.
> The nations all together are nothing for Him, insignificance itself and less than zero.
> So to whom will you compare God?
>
> (Isa. 40:12, 15–18)

A number of factors are usually cited for this change. They include a reckoning with the consequences of true monotheism: if there is indeed only one God in the universe, then He must rule over the affairs of all peoples—not just Israel. Such a God must be truly immerse. Even if these other nations are to be dismissed as a "drop from the bucket" (this is where our expression comes from)* and are as unimportant to Him as "dust on a scale" (that is, they weigh almost nothing)—nevertheless, they must figure in any overall picture of God's dominion. One who rules over such vast holdings is necessarily remote, like a great emperor who lives hundreds or even thousands of miles from most of his subjects. And it was not just monotheism that precipitated such a change. Certainly the more down-to-earth matters of Jerusalem's

* A "drop *from* the bucket" is the little bit of water that splashes out of the bucket as it is carried up from the river—a trivial amount not worth worrying about. "Drop *in* the bucket" is a misquotation.

capture by the Babylonians and the subsequent exile of the country's elite to Babylon for half a century had a role—there is nothing like exile to make one conscious of the existence of other nations and cultures and religions! If God truly is the God of all, if all *their* gods are vanity and nothingness, then He must also be the God of the Babylonians. Indeed, He must have been the one that ordered that the Babylonians win—which would make the Babylonian victory God's way of punishing Israel for its sins (as the Bible indeed maintains it was). But if so, then who but the mightiest, most cosmic deity could use a huge empire like Babylon as the "stick of His wrath" with which to beat Israel? And who but such a worldwide deity might then crush those same Babylonians fifty years later (to make the point that they were just a tool)—and crush them not by means of His people Israel, but using another surrogate, the king of the Medes and the Persians, "My servant Cyrus"?

This is the God, or close to the God, of later Judaism and Christianity—ungraspably big and far off, who rules the whole world and "calls off the generations" (Isa. 41:4) from His great remove in time and space. So much did this become our way of conceiving of God that the "other" God, who speaks to Moses face-to-face, the God into whom angels fade in biblical narrative, became an embarrassment to later theologians. It is, they said, really the great, universal God that these texts must have meant, the one who is omniscient and omnipresent and utterly unphysical. If they did not describe Him as such, well, they meant to—perhaps the Bible was just putting things in terms that were easily grasped by ordinary people.

But this, it seems to me, is not the conclusion suggested by the material examined thus far. Instead, a rather different way of approaching things suggests itself. Perhaps we would do better to think of the great omnipresent and omniscient God as a kind of model, like the models that scientists use as a way of talking about something that is not otherwise easily imagined or conceptualized. If this is so—and if, especially, this way of thinking about God emerged in the rather special geopolitical circumstances just described—then perhaps this other God, the theological embarrassment, should invite our renewed attention. He too is a model—or, I would rather say, a *report,* a report on the way things look, on the way it happens. Perhaps, in the end, all the things examined in this book—the angels, the absence of divine images, the victim's cry, the soul on its journey, and so forth—can fit together to create a rather different understanding.

ɞ ɞ ɞ

I hope to return to these matters presently. In the meantime, however, I should like to consider one last psalm that has some bearing on this question of God's presence and accessibility.

> O Lord, You search me out and know me.
> You know when I sit around or get up, You
> understand my thoughts from far off.
> You sift my comings and goings; You are familiar
> with all my ways.
> There is not one thing I say that You, Lord, do
> not know.
> In front and in back You press in on me and set
> Your hand upon me.
> Even things hidden from myself You know, things
> that are beyond me.

Not Searching for God

> Where can I go from Your spirit, or how can I get away from You?
> If I could go up to the sky, there You would be, or down to Sheol, there You are too.
> If I took up the wings of a gull to settle at the far end of the sea,
> even there Your hand would be leading me on,
> holding me in its grip.
> I might think, "At least darkness can hide me,
> nighttime will conceal me."
> But even darkness is not dark for You; night is as bright as the day, and light and dark are the same.
>
> (Ps. 139:1–12)

This psalm is not among the oldest in the Bible; most scholars would date it to the period after the Babylonian exile. It is relevant to the previous discussion because it is so clearly struggling with the matter of God's knowledge and God's place. Here we have to be careful. True, God is not confined to one place in this psalm—He does not simply reside in heaven or in His temple. At the same time, I think it would be inaccurate to say that even this psalm holds God to be everywhere, omnipresent. Such a thing certainly could be said in simple Hebrew, yet the psalm does not say it. Instead, it seems to present a deity who is, in some inexplicable way, both here and there (or able to zip around the universe so fast that the speaker cannot outrun Him): "If I could go up to the sky, there You would be, or down to Sheol, there You are too."

I might better demonstrate why this seems to fall short of divine omnipresence if I explain why the psalm also seems to fall short of claiming that God is omniscient. God does not know everything in this psalm (again, that He does could easily be said in Hebrew). What He can do is *find out* everything, probing a person's thoughts: "You search me out and know me." How exactly He does this is not said, but the psalm is clearly troubled by the idea that God might somehow enter or be present inside the human mind. That is why, having asserted that "You know when I sit around or get up," it quickly adds, "You understand my thoughts *from far off*." Are not the indicated words designed to tell us that God somehow is still "out there," a distinct being in the universe, but one who can, in some unexplained way, nonetheless have access to our innermost thoughts? It is for the same reason that I would hesitate to say that God is omnipresent in this psalm—if He were everywhere, then there would be no need for Him to understand anyone's thoughts from far off. He would be right there.

I think this psalm is highly significant precisely because of its brinksmanship: it seeks to present God as belonging to the world of the sun, pressing in on the human being from the outside, holding him in His hand, knowing his thoughts from afar—and yet it tries somehow to square all that with the reality of God's being as the psalmist knows it. And so, it is certainly no coincidence that, as it is bumping up against this paradox, the psalm leads us imperceptibly to the stark world of the soul. The lines that announce this entry are the last ones cited above, but they are not the last lines of the psalm.

> I might think, "At least darkness can hide me,
> nighttime will conceal me."

Not Searching for God

> But even darkness is not dark for You; night is as bright as the day, and light and dark are the same.

Here we are suddenly deep in pitch-darkness and bright, bright light. This is the land of the soul, the great inside (see Chapter 6)—and so quite naturally the psalm modulates from the sun world to deep inside:

> It was you who created my innards, You shaped me inside my mother's womb.
> I praise You for the wondrous way I was made, wondrous indeed is Your fashioning, and my soul knows it well.
> My frame was not hidden from You, though I was made in a secret place, knitted together at the bottom of the earth.
> Your eyes beheld my raw form, and everything is recorded in Your book, not a day of their making is missing.
> How dear to me are Your thoughts, God, how numerous their sums; if I tried to count them, they would outnumber the sand.
> When I wake up, I am still with You.
>
> (Ps. 139:13–18)

Having evoked the world of darkness and great light, the psalmist is transported into the starkness, that buzzing, electric world from which he glimpses the moment of his own creation. *You* did it, he says, and then (in lines that, were not the shoe on the other foot, one might rightly describe as Whitmanesque, right down to the untroubled repetition within them): "I praise You for the wondrous way I was made, wondrous indeed is Your fashioning, and my soul knows it well." But how can that be? If God is out there, out in the world, zipping from sky to Sheol, can He also be inside a human being, shaping the bones of a baby while it is still in its mother's womb? The question is troubling. But something pushes the psalmist to the unimaginable, and so he continues undaunted: I *know* You did it, I can feel that You were there. "My frame was not hidden from You, though I was made in a secret place, knitted together at the bottom of the earth." It is not clear whether "secret place" and the "bottom of the earth" are metaphorical references to the mother's womb or instead suggest that human beings all start off as some sort of prefab homunculus. In the end it probably does not matter. The point is that the psalmist is able to conceive of himself as he was back then—mere matter, *stuff,* waiting to be turned into a human being—and it is precisely at that moment that God came in: "Your eyes beheld my raw form, and everything is recorded in Your book." This is as far as the psalm can go: God is not only "out there" now, able to follow the psalmist to the farthest corners of the earth; He also knows the psalmist's every thought, reads them from far off. Indeed, He was there at the moment when raw matter became . . . himself. It all has to do with God's way with the world:

> How dear to me are Your thoughts, God, how
> numerous their sums; if I tried to count them, they
> would outnumber the sand.
> When I wake up, I am still with You.

Not Searching for God

These visionary lines end the journey. The soul is back home again.

It would be tempting (it has tempted others!) to leave the psalm off on this visionary note. But that is not where it ends. Instead, it fizzles back into the mundane requests that psalms so often end with. It is almost as if the dreamer now awake, suddenly remembers what a psalm is supposed to do and so turns to the great outside God with a request to crush his enemies:

> O God, if you would but slay the wicked, have the bloodthirsty depart from me!
> They invoke You on false pretenses. Your enemies swear falsely by You.
> You know I hate Your opponents, LORD; I take on any who go against You.
> I hate them altogether, they are my adversaries.
> Search me out, God, and know my heart; test me and know my thoughts.
> You can tell if my ways are troublesome. Guide me in the ways of e'er.
>
> (Ps. 139:19–24)

Even with this down-to-earth request, the psalmist cannot forget what he has seen, and so he returns to where he began. "Search me out, God, and know my heart" is meant to evoke the psalm's opening line, "O LORD, You search me out and know me." Since that is so, says the psalmist, You know that I am one of Yours, I am on Your side—so be on mine. But if that is the psalm's immediate conclusion, it is not, ultimately, what is significant for us. That real significance is in the soul's visionary journey, traveling from ordinary to extraordinary reality. This psalm, like the stories of angels with which we began, has a latch in it, a trapdoor. We thought we were in the outside world and then—whoops! It all turns out to have been something else entirely.

4

No Graven Images

The Ten Commandments, the Bible relates, were given to Moses on Mount Sinai. Some of their provisions are well known to everyone—commandments like "Honor thy father and thy mother" and "Thou shalt not kill." Somewhat less familiar, however, is their opening section:

> God spoke all these words: I am the LORD your God, who brought you out of the land of Egypt, the place of servitude.
>
> You shall not have any other gods besides Me.
>
> You shall not make for yourself any statue or the image of anything that is in the skies above or on the earth below or in the waters beneath the earth—you shall not bow down to them or worship them. For I am a jealous God. (Ex. 20:1–5)

These last lines, forbidding the making of images, have been the subject of much speculation among modern biblical scholars. To begin with, why should there have been any such prohibition—

what is wrong with making statues or pictures for purposes of worship? Theoretically, at least, such images might help the worshiper to focus his or her devotions, or at least afford a concrete representation for a hard-to-imagine, altogether spiritual entity. What is wrong with that?

From ancient times, people have sought the answer to this question in the words that immediately precede this prohibition of image making: "You shall not have any other gods besides Me." There is probably no coincidence in the juxtaposition of these two matters. Those other gods, we know, were indeed worshiped through images—these are the "molten gods" (Ex. 34:17; Lev. 19:4; Deut. 27:15; Hos. 13:2) or "gods of wood and stone" (Deut 4:28, 28:36, 29:17; 2 Kings 19:18; Isa. 37:19) denounced by so many biblical prophets. It would thus seem that the Bible's purpose in outlawing the making of such images was primarily to block off one easy way in which Israelites might be led into worshiping these other gods. That is, if they were to worship their own God through some image or statue, might they not at some point slip into worshiping another god who was conventionally represented by the same or some similar image? After all, many gods were represented by forms that would also have been appropriate to Israel's God—a statue of a mighty warrior brandishing heavenly weapons (see Ex. 15:3; Isa. 42:13), for example, or a benign father figure (Ex. 4:22; Deut. 14:1) surrounded by an awe-inspiring halo of light. Sometimes the power of gods and goddesses could also be represented by a wild animal with which they were associated, or by a solar disk, or by a weapon or a plow or some other tool. If any of these were connected with Israel's God, would that not suggest that He and these other deities were similar or even equivalent?

In fact, the words that immediately follow this prohibition of image making seem to return us to the subject of other gods. "For I am a jealous God," God asserts. Now, this phrase is used in two other places (Ex. 34:14; Deut. 6:15) in which God's jealousy is connected to one matter in particular: the prohibition of Israel's worshiping other deities. So it is probably no coincidence that these same words are used here. It is as if God were saying: Do not worship other gods; in fact, do not even worship Me with images that might someday lead you to worship other gods, because I just cannot put up with such a possibility, I am a jealous God.*

The matter would thus appear to be quite straightforward. Divine images were forbidden in Israel because of their connection with the gods of other nations. But that may not be all there is to it. The essence of this prohibition of divine images may go much deeper—in fact, it seems to be connected to another important aspect of the way that God was apprehended in biblical times. For as scholars have come to know lately, the gods elsewhere in the ancient Near East were not simply represented by images. They *were* the images. That is, the gods lived inside their own statues.

---

* Some modern translations read "I am a *zealous* God"; others have "an *impassioned* God" or the like. Whatever the translation, the point of this self-description is God's acknowledgment that what He has just said is somehow unusual and therefore, as it were, in need of explanation. That is, the gods of others peoples generally have no problem with sharing their people's devotions with other deities—polytheism is the "default setting" of the ancient Near East. But that is not the case with Me, God says—I am unusually touchy (*qannā'*) in this matter, I am a jealous God.

The God of Old

ɞ ɞ ɞ

Hollywood has popularized the figure of the flashlight-wielding archaeologist inspecting the ruins of ancient Egypt—and Egyptian religion is scarcely irrelevant to the study of biblical Israel. But Egypt is not the only place where those flashlights have been wielded, and for various reasons, Mesopotamian and Canaanite religious practices and beliefs seem in some important ways closer to those of ancient Israel; they also exercised a direct and long-lasting influence on Israel over time. For both these reasons, then, what archaeologists have turned up in modern-day Iraq and Syria can tell us much about the religious ideas of ancient Israelites.

Mesopotamia is the name the Greeks gave to the land between (and around) two great rivers, the Tigris and the Euphrates. Its territory corresponded roughly to that of the present state of Iraq. These two great rivers provided the region's earliest inhabitants with the advantages that great rivers often afford in a hot climate—a year-round supply of fresh drinking water for humans and animals, fertile land along the riverbank that can yield abundant crops despite the summer drought, and a steady means of transportation from one point to another along the river. These two rivers in particular are also famous for the succulent varieties of fish they yield up, some so fat that they can be fried in a pan without oil or butter—here was another attraction!

The oldest recorded Mesopotamian civilization is that of a people known as the Sumerians, who apparently immigrated there from elsewhere, probably from the southeast. To this day their origins remain obscure; they were not a Semitic people, indeed, their language is altogether unique and unrelated to any other known language on earth. But theirs was a highly sophisticated civilization, one that is credited with the invention of a unique writing system in which signs were made with a wedge-like tool sunk into wet clay (that is, cuneiform writing; the Latin *cuneus* means "wedge"). Crude texts using this writing system go back way before biblical Israel—to around 3200 B.C.E. Not only did the Sumerians use and gradually improve cuneiform, leaving us a record of their commercial and cultural life, but they also bequeathed it to other peoples who came to inhabit the same region, the Babylonians and the Assyrians, who modified it to fit their own needs.

The Sumerians thrived in Mesopotamia for a while. Their sophisticated urban culture flourished not least because of their development of a network of secondary canals off the two great rivers, which significantly expanded the area of arable lands. The planning and organization required for such an undertaking was considerable, and it served as a model for other peoples. Indeed, the Sumerian word *KU.GAL* (which for some reason I have always found unforgettable), meaning "irrigation supervisor," was one of the many Sumerian words that passed into Semitic languages, in this case not only Babylonian but Old Aramaic. But the Sumerians coexisted in the region with Semites from the "land of Akkad" farther north. These Akkadians were part of a larger Semitic population throughout the region, represented at an early stage in nearby Syria and elsewhere. They were presumably seminomads who grazed their sheep at the desert's edge and then gradually came to settle along the two rivers. Ultimately these Semites grew to outnumber the Sumerians; by the end of the third millennium B.C.E., they had basically absorbed both the Sumerians' civilization and their population within their own.

Mesopotamian history in the centuries that followed is a thing of rising and falling empires. The older form of social organization, the city-state, soon gave way to the multicity kingdom: a strong-armed monarch would succeed in imposing his rule on a chain of neighboring cities, thus creating a formidable military and economic bloc. The first such empire was that of Sargon the Great, king of Akkad around 2300 B.C.E. Sargon's empire lasted for a bit less than two centuries, but its breadth served as a model for later regimes. Hammurabi (descended from the West Semitic Amorites who had entered the region toward the end of Sargon's empire) propelled his kingdom, Babylon, to the forefront of Mesopotamian civilization in the early second millennium (1792–1750 B.C.E.). In later centuries, Babylon, in the south-central part of Mesopotamia, vied with Assyria in the north for overall control. The might of the neo-Assyrian empire was a formidable factor during much of biblical Israel's history; it stretched for a time from Iran in the east to today's Turkey in the northwest and southward through Israel and down as far as Egypt. It was this empire that was to conquer Israel's northern tribes in 722 B.C.E. and exile them to parts unknown, never to return (these are the "ten lost tribes"). Somewhat later, the emperor Ashurbanipal (668–627 B.C.E.) carried forward neo-Assyrian domination with his military might. Yet not long after his death, Assyria fell to the resurgent power in the south, the neo-Babylonian empire. Its greatest leader, Nebuchadnezzar II (604–562 B.C.E.), is famous in the Bible as the king who oversaw Jerusalem's conquest (587 B.C.E.) and the exile of its people to Babylon.

Such was Mesopotamia in ancient times. Our interest, however, is in the religion practiced by its inhabitants during this whole period, and especially in the statues and other images of their gods that they have left behind. These are not easy to interpret, although Mesopotamian religion has been studied intensively since the first important archaeological finds were made in the region in the nineteenth century. Part of the reason is that Mesopotamian religion was not a static thing: ideas about the gods and everything else underwent some fundamental changes over the course of three millennia. Understanding those changes is a notoriously difficult undertaking. On top of all of the difficulties of dating specific artifacts and texts in their different editions, and of taking into consideration not only all that has been excavated but, as well, the many significant things that, in all probability, have not—on top of all this there remains the greatest difficulty, and that is getting into the spirit of the texts and artifacts themselves. We live at a great remove from the conventions and basic understandings, the givens, of those distant times. If, as was suggested earlier, it is difficult for us today to enter the world of the Bible and its ancient texts, how much more difficult is it for us to enter the far older world represented by the most ancient writings and artifacts of Mesopotamia!

This is strikingly true with regard to the Mesopotamians' statues of their gods. Often, these images were not described or treated as mere *representations* of the gods; they were actually said to *be* the gods. At first this idea seems preposterous. How can a god—who by definition is some powerful mover in the world, causing crops to ripen or moving the sun or the moon through the sky—be inside a little wooden statue overlaid with precious metals and fine cloth, a statue small enough to be paraded through the streets or stuck in some ordinary-sized shrine somewhere? So preposterous did this notion seem that scholars for a long while rejected it, and along with it the Bible's critique of idol worship, which presented the worship of divine images in just these terms (for example, Isa. 44:9–20). Recently, however, more and more texts have come to light that say quite unequivocally that the gods were indeed there, inside their images, that the images actually *were* them. How could this be?

Part of the answer lies in the power that images have, or can have, in everyday life. We can see this at work in the array of images—toys—that we regularly give our children to play with. For example, this little girl has a doll—in fact, dolls and dolls. They are all her babies, she is proud to say, and she gives them names and dresses them and takes care of them. Often, she talks to them. Of course she "knows" they are not alive, but this knowledge seems to her quite inconsequential, and when she is alone you can sometimes overhear her scolding them or encouraging them to do something. Inconsequential too is the fact that most of the dolls are the wrong size, that is, there are not many among them that are actually baby-sized babies; in any case, she does not seem to give the realistic dolls any preference over the others. Some of the others—many, in fact—are actually miniature models of adults, one-fifth or one-tenth of what they would be in real life. Nor are these representations true to life in all but their size, often they have greatly exaggerated breasts and other feminine features. This bothers her not at all. What she wants is for their identity to be clear so that she can interact with them in here, on her own turf and terms, with herself in charge; for that purpose they are just perfect.

Similarly, her brother has toy cars, and they too have an imagined life. He makes them go along the floor, crashes one into another while making a crashing sound in his own mouth—for him all this is happening somewhere real. It is, to be precise, a world in which *he* makes the cars come and go very much as adults do on the road outside his window. He has another toy, however, and this one is particularly relevant to our subject: a little plastic replica of Superman. He likes to hold it from the bottom and make it fly through the air, its cape fluttering in the wind just like the Superman of the movies. He can spend long minutes doing this, fascinated. Of course, he will agree that what he holds in his hand is not the real Superman, but he may say this just to be agreeable. After all, what is more real, a three-dimensional image that you can actually hold in your hand, or a two-dimensional image that flickers for a few moments on a distant screen? And why is "real" any kind of important quality anyway? Like his sister, he wants to interact with this being from the world out there, but interact with it in here. He knows what Superman does, what a great hero he is, and now here Superman is, undeniably so, in his hand, wearing just the right clothes and colors—what does reality have to do with anything?

Of course, something in us rebels. That is *not* Superman, the dolls are *not* real, the toy cars will not move on their own. But suppose—and this is, admittedly, not easy—that we could put those sentiments aside for a moment in the interests of something higher, some metaphysical project: the gods.

The gods exist, of course—every ancient Mesopotamian knew that. Divinity was simply obvious, axiomatic. It was there long before the first humans even began to think in some fashion about the nature of their own existence and how they fit into the world, that is, about what humans can and cannot do. But once humans did begin to contemplate such things, the existence of divine *causers,* unseen movers, seemed to impose itself on their thought. After all, things in this world usually do not just happen; *someone* makes them happen. Yet, in the case of a crafty human, or a particular bird's cry, the connection between action and result is not always obvious; sometimes the one who causes things, or the way in which he causes them, is hidden. How much more likely was this to be the case for the great things that go on in the world, the ripening of crops and the change of seasons, the movement of the sun and moon and stars! Surely someone, or a host of great *someones* (because there are so many things that move and change), was at work. Indeed, this coterie of unseen powers, invisible causers, must stand behind *all* the unexplained changes that one sees.

The human apprehension of divinity had, as mentioned, begun long before (though this may be hard for us to imagine): but once it came to focus on these powerful beings, the gods, the connection between the two became automatic and self-evident. Henceforth, the human soul would be fixed upon, and shaped by, the existence of these unseen doers. So, of course, people invoked the gods, implored the gods, named their own children after gods ("Marduk-have-mercy-on-me," "Ishtar-is-heaven's-queen," "Guard-me-Shamash"); and even when people were not consciously thinking about the gods, they nonetheless lived every minute of their daily lives in the gods' shadow. The gods were there, unseen, just beyond our reach, and they were very great, while we humans were, and still are, very small.

But what were the gods like? Well—a Mesopotamian might have said—we are human and they, of course, are not. And yet, when you think about it, they must be somewhat, or even very much, like us. After all, unlike the animals, we use our clever hands to make things happen in our world—the gods could scarcely do without hands themselves. They must also have mouths and tongues to speak with—for surely they are not dumb like the animals, but talk with one another as we do. And undoubtedly they also have eyes to see with, ears to hear with, and feet and bodies and sexual organs and everything else that we humans have in order to function in our world. In short, it seemed only logical that they look a great deal like humans. And then there was what the gods did, how they behaved. Humans relate to one another in the complex ways that they do—with struggles for power, friendships and spats, alliances and marriages, hierarchies and governments and councils. Could anything less be expected of the gods? So it was very difficult to imagine these great *causers,* in the sky or under the earth, as anything other than divine humanoids of some sort, going about their grand-scale business very much as people go about their own petty affairs.

Where were the gods to be found? They were of course "out there," up there or perhaps somewhere underneath us. Yet it would be wrong to think of them as diffuse, wholly theoretical entities, spread about the world homogeneously, like oxygen. They were actual beings with bodies, bodies (as we have just seen) not unlike our own. The main differences between gods and people were those of place and power. The gods lived in their own domain, on a kind of upper shelf, from which they performed the functions that they performed, things that were beyond a normal human's reach or control. They certainly affected human life, but in so doing they did not actually need to interact directly with humans very much. And the gods were supremely powerful. Thus, if it happened that a human being did encounter a god, he was not confronted with a faceless, inscrutable force. He was more like a modern person standing in front of a policeman: physically, you and the policeman are not too different, not of vastly different sizes, and yet the policeman has all the power. He can decide to arrest you if he wants and put you in jail for a time; he may even take out his gun and kill you. This may not be fair, but you are very careful with him nonetheless; you call him "Officer" and hope that he will simply leave you alone. The gods similarly inspired respect and fear; no one would seek to be in their company for any length of time or have a relationship with a god—that was too frightening, too dangerous. But being in contact with the gods had a potentially positive side nonetheless: they could take account of you and use their great power to change your existence for the better, bring you health or prosperity, lift the drought, foil the siege, turn everything around. And so, frightening as it was, the human beings eventually did seek out some controlled way to bring the gods down, to invite them to sojourn in the humans' midst and be served and adored and beseeched down here. If we make the surroundings comfortable enough and magnificent enough, they thought, if our priests offer them the choicest of our precious livestock and flocks and fill their palace with the scent of our sweetest incense, and if we build this prospective god–home on our highest mountain so that the heaven dwellers will not have far to travel, perhaps they will indeed consent to come and sojourn in our midst. Thus was born the ancient Near Eastern temple, in an age before the dawn of history.

We come, finally, to the matter of *how* the gods were actually present. Here, perhaps, we should think back to the little girl's dolls. What we consider realism, the representation of a baby-sized, babylike baby apparently does not speak to her, or does not speak to her any more than some other kind of doll. What she wants is to interact with a clearly identified being, or a bunch of beings, that she knows from elsewhere, from the real world, but interact with them here on her own terms, in a special world of her own fashioning. Similarly, to interact with the god, it was necessary to create a special world—the condensed, time-stopped eternity of the temple—and then actually to give the god a shape, a presence, within that world. The god's statue did not *symbolize* him or represent him; it was more than that; it needed to be more than that. For this purpose the humans did not have to make the god's statue huge, but merely to equip it with the face and limbs that they knew the god must have, and then, somehow, allow the thing that they fashioned to be inhabited, to become him-among-us. It may seem paradoxical, but it was precisely the small size of the statue and its unrealistic, low-tech representation that would allow the god to become infused in it, until the statue truly contained and *was* him.

A crude, spindly little statue invokes and invites. You stare and stare at it and after a while you can almost imagine that *he* is there, looking at you through the eyes of the statue; then, perhaps, you can reverse the process and reach back to him through his image.

When the statue of Marduk/Enlil, the supreme deity of Babylon, was carried from the silent peace of his temple shrine out into the bustling streets of the capital (which happened only twice a year, on the eighth day of the first and seventh months, that is, the spring and fall New Year's festivals), the townspeople crowded the parade route, pushing one another aside in an attempt to reach the statue, to kiss its feet, because *this was the god,* and doing so might assure his good favor in the months to come. Meanwhile, other people, priests or sages, studied the statue's face, because they knew that he was actually behind it, in it, and the slight changes in the way his face looked were a sign of what he was thinking and planning for the future:

> When Marduk, leaving the Esagila temple at the beginning of the year, has an open mouth—Enlil will raise his voice in anger against the land.
>
> When Marduk has his eyes closed—the land's inhabitants will feel sadness
>
> When Marduk has a somber face—famine will take hold of the countries.
>
> When Marduk has a face that shines—Enlil will make the land shine forever.

The god was inside the image; if you looked closely, you could see its features move.

But certainly rational people must have known that the statue was simply that, a statue, the product of human industry. Or did they? There is a group of ancient Mesopotamian texts that describe the production of divine statues. The image was indeed fashioned by human artisans, but then it was said to be "born," brought to life. After that it was clothed, given weapons and a crown, and last, surrounded with a *melammu,* a kind of halo of power that radiated outward to the beholder. While it was being shaped, it was indeed a statue, the image of Marduk, and it was so called. But once finished, it was not called an image; now it was Marduk himself. Indeed, the newly minted god was pointedly described as having been "born in heaven" and not, apparently, fashioned on earth: henceforth, the texts said, "you are counted [with the gods,] your brothers."

No Graven Images

The question of the extent to which divine images were truly believed to *be* the gods they depicted continues to intrigue scholars; it is never easy to distinguish doctrine from actual belief. But the claim that the image was the god certainly was made, and frequently. Particularly striking is the evidence from a certain Mesopotamian ritual, one that served both to purify a newly made divine image and, simultaneously, to disconnect that image from its human fashioners. The ceremony is know as *mīs pî* ("washing of the mouth"), along with the related *pit-pî* ("opening the mouth"). The disconnection part is particularly revealing. After the image had been completed, the priest would take the goldsmith's hands and symbolically cut them off with a wooden sword. Thus, this craftsman could not be the one who made this statue—he had no hands! The goldsmith would then intone a standardized, solemn oath: "In truth, the god X [various gods are named in different versions of the ritual], patron of [gold]smiths, has made him. I did not make him." The same assertion was made by the other artisans: they had, they said, nothing to do with its creation. It came from the gods. Henceforth, the texts said, it was the god.

ɕ ɕ ɕ

Where exactly the people of Israel first came from is still a matter of scholarly speculation and dispute. The book of Genesis and other biblical texts agree in saying that Israel's ancestors immigrated into the land of Canaan from elsewhere—in fact from Mesopotamia, according to some passages. Abraham's father, Terah, is thus said to have inhabited the city of Ur, a site that was at one time at the southern tip of Mesopotamia, where the two great rivers almost meet. At a certain point Terah decides to leave

Ur with his family: "Terah took his son Abram [Abraham], his grandson Lot the son of Haran, and his daughter-in-law Sarai, the wife of his son Abram, and they set out together from Ur of the Chaldeans for the land of Canaan" (Gen. 11:31). The book of Joshua similarly reports: "In olden times your forefathers, Terah, the father of Abraham and father of Nahor, lived beyond the Euphrates, and they worshiped other gods. But I [God] took your father Abraham from beyond the Euphrates and led him through the whole land of Canaan and multiplied his offspring" (Josh 24:2–3).

It is all the more remarkable, therefore, that the Bible elsewhere is quite emphatic in denying any connection between the civilizations of Mesopotamia and that of Israel (although in certain matters some resemblance is undeniable). One of the clearest of such statements is the well-known story of the Tower of Babel:

> The whole earth was of a single language and one set of words. As people migrated from the east, they came to a valley in the land of Shinar and settled there. Then they said to each other, "Let us make bricks and harden them with fire"—since bricks were like building-stones for them, and bitumen like mortar—and they said "Let us build a city for ourselves, with a tower that reaches the sky, so that we can make a name for ourselves and will not be scattered all over the land's surface." But the LORD came down to look at the city and tower that the people had built. Then the LORD said: "It is because they are a single people and have one language for everyone that they have been able to undertake this. Now nothing that they propose to do will be beyond their means! Let us go down and confuse

> their speech, so that they will not understand what they are saying to each other." Thus the LORD scattered them from there all over the land's surface, and the building of the city was stopped. That is why it is called Babel, because there the LORD confused the speech of the whole earth, and from there the LORD scattered them all over the earth's surface. (Gen. 11:1–9)

If one reads this story with an open mind, a question occurs immediately: what did the people do that was so wrong? Apparently all they wanted to do was build a city so that they could all live together. What was so bad about that? (The tower that they planned to build within the city is not unimportant, but neither is it the whole point of the story, as has often been asserted. After all, the end of the story says that "the building of the city was stopped," but what happened to the tower itself is not mentioned: apparently, this was of no great concern. It was the Bible's first interpreters who made so much of the tower, presenting it as a terrible act of human hubris—but they did so precisely so as to supply an answer to the great, unanswered question: what was wrong with the people's desire to build a city?)

It is certainly true that the story offers an explanation for the existence of different languages—more specifically, different *Semitic* languages, such as Hebrew, Aramaic, and Babylonian, which, despite their obvious communality, were mutually incomprehensible. But the confusion of tongues is not the whole point of this brief episode either. As scholars have long understood, much of the story's point lies in its attitude toward a particular civilization, that of Babylon. The tower in the story is a typical *ziqqurat,* a man-made, multistoried sanctuary such as was built in different Mesopotamian cities. Indeed, the name of the country in which the story takes place is pointedly explained by the narrative as coming from the Hebrew word *balal,* "confuse": Babylon (Hebrew *babel*) was so called, the story says, because it was there that God confused human speech and created different languages. To put it plainly, the story seems out to attack everything that characterized ancient Mesopotamian society. It is the Babylonian way of life that God rejects in the story. Babylonian city building, indeed empire building, resulting in massive conglomerations of people ("so that we will not be scattered all over the land's surface" is the people's justification for building the city) and the complex urban culture that it made possible, with its sophisticated temples and clergy and rituals—all this, the story seems to be saying, is a lot of bunk. Cities themselves are bunk.

The implications of this blunt assertion are not, I think, always appreciated sufficiently. It says much about ancient Israel in its perceived relationship to Mesopotamia at an early stage of its history. Those Eastern sophisticates are all wrong, the story says. The path of Israel, out in the far less developed, spread-out civilization of the Semitic hinterland, is the right one. "Israel's way is simple but true; it is not a lot of bunk." In this one may hear not only a rejection of the urban culture of Mesopotamia but a rejection of it in favor of something that could hardly even be thought to compete with it, something altogether humble and stripped down. This something stood in opposition not only to the Mesopotamian city, of course, but to its *ziqqurats* and its whole way of worshiping its gods. Israel's God, the story says, does not approve of that mumbo jumbo, the complicated temple architecture and all those omen watchers and diviners that function within it. He does not approve of it even in your territory; that is why, long ago, He came down to overthrow the building of your greatest city.

Situating this mentality in the development of Israelite religion is no easy task, but it seems to be of a piece with other things observed long ago by biblical scholars—for example, the contrast between the complex building techniques and skills practiced elsewhere in the Near East and the Bible's ancient prohibition of even using a simple tool to quarry or shape the stones of an altar (Ex. 20:25), or the contrast between the blunt, apodictic laws found in some parts of the Bible ("Keep the sabbath. Honor your parents. Do not murder") and the more complicated casuistic law ("If such-and-such should be the case, and such-and-such should next ensue, then . . .") characteristic of the Mesopotamian legal idiom (and found as well in other parts of Bible).

The Bible's prohibition of divine images seems to belong to the same mentality. It bespeaks a time of beginning, or perhaps more accurately, a time of starting over from the beginning, and of Israel's being found better than Babylon not for having competed with its sophistication but for having rejected it. Opposed to those canals and densely packed cities and allied townships are these great, whistling, open spaces on the other side of the desert, dotted here and there with crude outposts and open-air worship sites with altars made of ordinary dirt or simple, unhewn stones. It is here that people bow down to an unusual God, one who refuses to take up residence in a craftsman's images.

ര ര ര

The antiquity of the Bible's prohibition of divine images has sometimes been questioned. Some modern researchers have argued that the texts in which this prohibition appears either are not among the Bible's earliest or must have undergone some later revision. One of the arguments in support of this contention is that some apparently ancient biblical texts do talk about divine images without any disapproval. Thus, Rachel steals her father's teraphim, evidently some kind of sacred image (Gen. 31:19; see also Jdg. 17:5; Ezek. 21:21; Zech. 10:2); the text of Genesis implies no criticism of her father, Laban, for having had them, nor any of Rachel for taking them. The book of Judges (chapters 17 and 18) likewise relates how Micah possessed a "graven image and a molten image"—presumably these too were objects of veneration. However, in neither case is it said that these were actual images of Israel's God (that is, the deity known in the Bible as "the LORD" [YHWH]). Some scholars now believe that teraphim were actually images of departed ancestors. Whatever the case, there is ample archaeological and literary evidence to suggest that ancient Israelites sometimes worshiped other gods and goddesses along with the LORD—prophetic texts criticize the practice, to be sure, but that only strengthens the likelihood of it having once been widespread. If so, narratives that reflect such behavior may not tell us much about official doctrine or when it originated. Furthermore, in the two stories mentioned, the objects themselves were apparently not items of *public* worship but private devotion. The whole realm of private worship—particularly as an aspect of popular religion in biblical times—is only now beginning to be explored; it is therefore difficult at this stage to draw any firm conclusions. But some distinction certainly may have existed between the use of images in the public and the private sphere. With all these uncertainties, then, there is really no firm basis for concluding that the mention of images in passages such as these narratives in Genesis and Judges disprove the antiquity of the image-making prohibition with regard to Israel's God.

Potentially more troubling is the bronze serpent that Moses himself is ordered to create in Numbers 21, since it was clearly a *public* cultic object in the Jerusalem temple for some years—until the time of King Hezekiah, when, the Bible reports, it was destroyed. Was it an image of the God of Israel? Certainly that possibility is not to be excluded. The Bible itself does not say that, of course. The bronze serpent is instead described as serving a healing function ("And so it happened that if someone was bitten by a snake, he would look at the bronze serpent and live"—Num. 21:9). But how ancient Israelites actually came to conceive of it may be better represented by the brief mention of the same bronze serpent in 2 Kings 18:4. There it is implied that the serpent was indeed an object of veneration ("for until that time the Israelites had been offering sacrifices to it"). It adds, however, that the serpent had a name, Nehushtan (roughly, "Bronzy"). This is certainly not a divine name or epithet, and its very existence seems once again to argue against the idea that the serpent was held to be an image of Israel's God. One further point should be mentioned. In Mesopotamian society, which, as we have glimpsed briefly, had some historical connections with that of Israel, animals and inanimate objects were indeed sometimes *associated* with a deity, as symbols of their power, but images of the gods themselves were invariably in the shape of humans and not animals. This distinction between symbols and images is not always easy to make, of course, but it is nonetheless important. The same distinction apparently held in ancient Canaan. On balance, then, the case of the bronze serpent does not seem to tell us anything unambiguous about how old the prohibition of divine images in Israel might be.

The fact that the bronze serpent was destroyed in the days of Hezekiah along with other religiously dubious items (2 Kings 18:4) is widely understood to show that his time (the late eighth to early seventh century B.C.E.) was one of religious reform. This fact itself may offer some further illumination. For we know that reformers often choose to take some earlier provision or practice—preferably one that has been neglected, or at least not observed as stringently as is logically possible—and turn it into a major issue: "Look at how lax my opponents (or predecessors) were in this important matter!" If something like this is what happened in the days of Hezekiah, then that would suggest that some sort of prohibition of cultic images had indeed existed since olden times, but that it underwent a revival or at least some increased stringency in Hezekiah's own day.

Whatever one think of the Bible's own evidence about the prohibition of divine images, there is one fairly indisputable archaeological fact to consider. To date, not a single anthropomorphic statue of Israel's God has turned up at any of the very numerous cultic sites excavated within the confines of biblical Israel (or outside of it, for that matter). Some of these excavated cultic sites go back to the earliest periods of Israel's existence, and the absence of any anthropomorphic representation of God there must thus be treated with the greatest seriousness. It suggests that, whatever a few scattered literary references may or may not imply (and even a real cultic statue or two, if it should ever turn up), some sort of taboo of such images of God probably did exist and was observed from very early times. This is hardly a negligible piece of information, especially since it puts ancient Israel in such sharp contrast with Mesopotamia. And not just Mesopotamia.

ɞ ɞ ɞ

If Israel's sacred book portrays Mesopotamian civilization in negative terms, it is scarcely more generous when it comes to that of the Canaanites, the original inhabitants of Israel's land and that of their immediate neighbors. On the contrary, everything about the Canaanites is apparently reprehensible. For example, the narratives concerning Israel's immediate male ancestors, Abraham, Isaac, and Jacob, are in accord that a Canaanite woman could never have been a proper mate for any of them. Abraham thus has his servant take a solemn oath to promise that "you will not take a wife for my son from the daughters of the Canaanites among whom I dwell" (Gen. 24:4)—and he then dispatches the servant out of the country to find a bride for Isaac. Later, Rebekah (the bride whom the servant found) sounds a similar note with her husband, Isaac: "I am disgusted with my life at the thought of the Hittite [here, Canaanite] women. If [our son] Jacob marries a Hittite woman like these, from among the native women, how can I go on living?" Isaac concurs and instructs Jacob, "You shall not take a wife from among the Canaanite women" (Gen. 27:46–28:1). Note that this injunction had nothing to do with marrying outside of Israel—there was no Israel yet, and in any case, other, later Israelites marry Egyptians, Arameans, or Mesopotamians with no apparent disapproval expressed in the text. What was so bad about Canaanites? These texts do not bother to say—perhaps it was simply obvious.

Those ancestral narratives do not point, even indirectly, to

Canaanite religious practices as the problem, but that was certainly said elsewhere in the Bible: "You shall not intermarry with them [the seven Canaanite nations]: do not give your daughters to their sons or take their daughters for your sons. For they will turn your children away from Me to worship other gods, and the LORD's anger will blaze forth against you and He will promptly destroy you. Instead, this is what you shall do to them: tear down their altars, smash their pillars, cut down their sacred posts, and consign their images to fire" (Deut. 7:3–5). Similar disgust at Canaanite religion is expressed elsewhere: "When My angel goes before you and brings you to the Amorites, the Hittites, the Perizzites, the Canaanites, the Hivites, and the Jebusites, and I annihilate them, you shall not bow down to their gods in worship or follow their practices, but shall tear them down and smash their pillars to bits. You shall serve the LORD your God, and He will bless your bread and your water" (Ex. 23:23–24). Time and again, in fact, the Israelites are commanded to destroy every remnant of Canaanite religious practice. What the Canaanites believed and did is described as "horrible" and the principal reason for which the land "vomited" them from its midst.

To read such things, one might well conclude that the civilization of Israel had absolutely nothing to do with that of the Canaanites. And yet, modern scholars know a different story. Archaeologists have found great continuity between the building styles and artifacts of Canaanites and Israelites in the Late Bronze Age—they seem to bespeak a common material culture. This similarity extends even to the Bible's description of the structures in which the Israelites worshiped, such as the great temple that Solomon is said to have built in Jerusalem. Of course, the Bible itself recounts that this temple was built with materials and artisans supplied by the Phoenician/Canaanite King Hyram of Tyre (1 Kings 5:2–10)—perhaps that explains why the sacred Jerusalem sanctuary in many ways resembled a typical West Semitic temple. Archaeologists have found many striking similarities between the Bible's description of the Jerusalem temple and two excavated models, the temples found at ʿEin Daraʿ (tenth to eighth century B.C.E.) and Tel Taʿyinat (eighth century B.C.E.), both in modern Syria.

But the resemblance goes beyond that of buildings and artifacts: it reaches to matters still more fundamental. Much of our current knowledge of the religion and culture of Israel's Canaanite neighbors has been gleaned from the chance discovery of a great library of texts at ancient Ugarit (a site in coastal Syria called nowadays Ras Shamra). The Ugaritic texts, first unearthed in 1928, are written in a language strikingly similar to biblical Hebrew. In fact, Ugaritic and Hebrew are arguably two dialects of the same basic tongue. To be sure, Ugarit lay far to the north of biblical Israel (the site excavated at Ras Shamra is about one hundred miles north of present-day Beirut). To the extent that they can even be called Canaanites, the people of Ugarit were certainly not the Canaanites next door. Moreover, Ugarit was separated chronologically from biblical Israel: the works in its library were composed sometime in the Late Bronze Age, between around 1550 and 1200 B.C.E., well before Israel's emergence as a nation. Despite these differences, Ugaritic and Israelite writings have a lot in common. Biblical poetry in the Psalms and elsewhere is written in a style that is sometimes very reminiscent of Ugaritic, with the same images and even the same phrases recurring in both. Ugaritic and biblical Hebrew also share some common terms for the various classes of sacrifices that were offered in temples, as well as common terms for temple personnel.

Even more striking are the resemblances between the gods of Ugarit and some aspects of God as presented in the Hebrew Bible. For example, the head of the Ugaritic pantheon is called El, and this same name is often used of Israel's God (translated, along with the Hebrew word *Elohim,* as "God" in most Bibles). Many of the things that are said of El in Ugaritic—that he is an ancient and wise father figure who presides over the divine council and metes out justice and mercy to human beings—are said as well of God in the Bible. In the Ugaritic texts El has a colleague, a younger, more vigorous god called Baal ("Master") and he too bears some resemblance to biblical depictions of God. Indeed, a few scattered biblical texts seem to imply that "Baal" was another epithet for Israel's God. (For example, the personal name Bealyah appears in 1 Chr. 12:6, and the personal name Yehobaal appears on an excavated seal—both these seem to imply that Baal was at one time a name or epithet for God; see also Hos. 2:16, perhaps also Isa. 1:3, and such Israelite names as Jerubbaal [for Gideon], Jdg. 7:1). Baal was an important god at Ugarit, the storm god who brought the life-giving rain. Some of the same things that he is said to do—send forth thunder and lightning or defeat the dragon and sea monster Yamm—are said in the Bible of Israel's God (see Ps. 29, 74:13–14, 104:6–9; Job 26:12, 38:8–11; Isa. 27:1). Indeed, the Psalms at one point refer to Israel's God as the "cloud rider" (Ps. 68:4)—precisely the same phrase is used of Baal at Ugarit.

What is one to make of such evidence? Neighboring civilizations can, of course, influence one another, sometimes quite unconsciously, and this influence may extend to matters of religion. Indeed, scholars are familiar with the phenomenon known as syncretism, whereby the god of religion X is identified with another god from religion Y; or X's god is worshiped in some ceremony derived from religion Y. This happened a great deal in the ancient world, and items such as the "Hanukkah bush," adopted by some American Jews in imitation of the Christmas tree, or the recent espousal of a very Christian-style messianism by a group of Hasidic Jews, show that syncretism is not dead in our own time. One might therefore seek to explain the resemblances between Canaanite and Israelite religious terminology and artifacts and even beliefs as an extended example of such syncretism. But some scholars have taken a more far-reaching approach and suggested that the religion of Israel's ancestors was originally altogether like that of other inhabitants of Canaan, devoted to the worship of El and other Canaanite gods. It was only at some point in history that a new God—the God of the Bible, known specifically by the Hebrew letters Y-H-W-H—entered the land of Canaan from the south and east, and He became the God of the future people of Israel. In a sense, these scholars say, the worship of this God was grafted onto existing ideas and terminology and even modes of worship, so that Israel's God was in many ways described and venerated in the same way as El and Baal and even identified with them. At the same time, His adherents would have distanced themselves utterly from others in Canaan. Their God demanded exclusive loyalty—"You shall have no other gods besides Me"—and in this they kept themselves distinct from their neighbors the Canaanites.

Such contentions are, by the nature of things, rarely given to absolute proof. But what is particularly intriguing for the present discussion is the whole connection of this theory with the making of divine images. For image making was one item on which Israelite and Canaanite religious practices appear to have differed sharply. The Canaanites, like the Mesopotamians, certainly had anthropomorphic cultic images, whereas, as we have seen, the literary and archaeological evidence suggests that Israelites sought to avoid them for Israel's God. Whatever other connections might have existed between Canaanites and Israelites, this was a clear dividing line: as the Ten Commandments attest, the God of the Israelites commanded them not to make images of Him.

ɞ ɞ ɞ

One aspect of God's nature has been highlighted in an earlier chapter: He appears to people. He appears to Abraham at Mamre, to Jacob at Bethel, and to Moses on Mount Horeb. He appears as an angel to Joshua and to Manoah's wife and to Gideon and to many other individuals. He also appears to all of Israel at Mount Sinai (Ex. 19–20), and to the people as a whole many times thereafter. In fact, God's being seen by people is something that is talked about throughout the Bible. He appears to David (2 Chr. 3:1) and to Solomon at Gibeon (1 Kings 3:5). Isaiah sees Him in the sanctuary (Isa. 6). "The Lord revealed Himself to me [*or* "to him"] long ago," Jeremiah says (Jer. 31:2). Biblical texts do not seem at all reluctant to report such things. "The Lord appeared to Abram," the book of Genesis reports in yet another place, "and he built an altar there to the Lord who appeared to him" (Gen. 12:7). "God Almighty appeared to me in Luz, in the land of Canaan," says Jacob, reviewing earlier events, "and He blessed me" (Gen. 48:3). The psalmist says, "My soul thirsts for the living God, for the time when I may go and see God's face" (Ps. 42:2). When Moses expresses doubts about the Israelites' willingness to follow him, he says, "They will not believe me or do what I say. Instead they will say, 'The LORD did not appear to you' " (Ex. 4:1). Apparently, if God had not appeared to him, the Israelites would be right not to follow Moses. Later, Moses says: "You, O LORD, are in the midst of this people, and You *are seen by them eye to eye,* and Your cloud stands above them, and in a pillar of cloud You go before them by day, and in a pillar of fire by night" (Num. 14:14). Dozens of other examples could be cited.

Modern readers feel some discomfort at all this. After all, God does not appear nowadays, and a number of other biblical texts (as well as almost all of postbiblical theology) suggest that God cannot be seen at all. Certainly, we feel, God has no body or physical substance that can be viewed. There is thus a tendency for people to sweep under the rug biblical passages that talk about *seeing* God; these passages cannot mean what they seem to be saying. Scholastics, medieval theologians, and modern writers have all followed this line of thought. Even today's hard-nosed biblical scholars—bent on studying biblical texts in their original historical context and without theological blinders—sometimes have a tendency to shy away from this God–who–appears. Many standard discussions of theophany (the phenomenon of God appearing to humans) focus not on the passages mentioned but on others, in which God is manifest in a storm like the Canaanite Baal (Habakkuk 3; Psalm 29) or in great earthly or cosmic upheaval (Psalm 68 and the like); He is thus viewed by humans in some mediated fashion and at some distance. These passages certainly exist—but that is hardly all there is to God's appearing.

The God of Old

One of the most striking things about God's appearances to human beings is that they are often presented in biblical narratives as the climactic moment, the culmination of a whole story or incident. So it was with Manoah, for example: the couple's encounter with the man of God ends when the man's true identity is revealed and Manoah says, "We shall surely die, for we have seen God." Jacob's encounter with a man similarly culminates with his realization that "I have seen God face to face." Gideon's meeting likewise ends with Gideon saying, "O LORD God! I have seen the angel of the LORD face to face." So it is as well in the story of the binding of Isaac; after Isaac's life is spared, the narrative says: "And the name of the place was called 'The LORD is seen,' as it is said today, 'The LORD is seen on the mountain.'"* Another such culminating moment occurs in Exodus, when God concludes his great covenant with the Israelites. A delegation of

---

* The traditional translation of Gen. 22:14 is: "And the name of the place was called 'The Lord sees,' as it is said to day, 'The Lord is seen on the mountain." But this translation is problematic because of an apparent inconsistency. If the place was called "The Lord sees," then the continuation should be, "as it is said today, 'The Lord *sees* on the mountain.' " Because of ambiguities in the Hebrew writing system, the words "see" and "is seen" are actually written with the same letters (although they are pronounced differently). Thus it is impossible to know whether both verbs are to be read as "is seen" or as "sees," or whether indeed one is to be read one way and the other the other way (as the traditional translation has it). There are good arguments to make for reading both as "sees" (see Gen. 22:8, where the Lord *sees*); nevertheless, it seems more likely to me that the mountain was known as a sacred site because the Lord *is seen* there rather than because he *sees* there—for certainly even the oldest biblical texts hold that God *sees* from the heavens and in all sorts of places on earth.

Israelites offers sacrifices, and the "blood of the covenant" is sprinkled on all the participants. Then

> Moses and Aaron, Nadab and Abihu, and seventy of the elders of Israel went up, and they saw the God of Israel. Under his feet there was something like a pavement of sapphire, like the very heavens for purity. And He [God] did not harm the leaders of Israel. They beheld God, and they ate and they drank. (Ex. 24:9–11)

There are, of course, passages that seem to pull in the other direction. When, in Exodus 33, Moses asks to see God's "glory" (His physical being or presence). God answers, "No man can see me and live"—although He does go on to reveal himself to Moses "from behind." The book of Deuteronomy stresses that God was manifest at Mount Sinai in the form of a fire, but that the Israelites saw no distinct image of Him: "And the LORD spoke to you from amidst the fire; you could hear the sound of the words [He spoke], but you saw no image, except for the sound" (Deut. 4:12). The existence of such passages is certainly interesting, but they hardly upset the evidence already cited. Certainly a great many biblical texts say that God *was* seen; indeed, they seem to celebrate that fact and make of it the culmination of the whole episode.

(I should add that while some later biblical texts do demonstrate a reluctance to refer to God being seen, this way of conceiving of Him was nonetheless extraordinarily long-lived. Philo of Alexandria, the Hellenistic Jewish philosopher of the first century, repeatedly says that Israel was so named because this name signifies *'ish ra'ah* [or *ro'eh*] *'El,* "a man seeing God." In rabbinic writings from the second to the sixth centuries C.E., God is frequently represented as having appeared to human beings, sometimes in altogether human dimensions. Thus, a famous interpretive tradition asserts that the words "This is my God" in Ex. 15:2 indicate that all of Israel, from Moses to the lowliest maidservant, attained a level of prophetic sight greater than that of Ezekiel, since they saw God so clearly that they could point to Him and say "this." An earlier or contemporaneous tradition takes a phrase in Deut. 4:34, *mora'im gedolim,* "great frights," as if it read instead "great sights," commenting, "This is the revelation of the divine presence." Time and again, God is presented in rabbinic texts as appearing in human form—indeed, this is one of that literature's most striking traits.)

One detail that sometimes marks such appearances is particularly telling. The biblical text seems to stress the faculty of sight itself, almost as if to say, "This was not ordinary seeing, but *seeing*":

> And God heard the boy's voice [crying] and an angel of God called out from heaven and said to her [Hagar], "What is the matter, Hagar? Do not be afraid, because God has heard the boy's crying where he is. Come, pick the boy up again and hold him tight, for I will make him into a great nation." *And God opened her* [*Hagar's*] *eyes,* and she saw a well of water. (Gen. 21:17–19)

There is nothing visionary about the well that Hagar sees—she proceeds to fill up her canteen with real water from it. No, what "God opened her eyes" means here is that God caused Hagar to break out of the "fog" and understand what had just happened, what it was that she was really seeing. Similarly:

> Then *the LORD opened Balaam's eyes* and he saw the angel of the LORD standing in the way. (Num. 22:31)

> Then Manoah took the goat and the grain offering, and offered them up to the LORD on a rock, and something wondrous happened while Manoah and his wife were watching. As the flames were rising up from the altar toward the sky, the angel of the LORD rose up in the flames of the altar. *And Manoah and his wife saw,* and they fell on their faces to the ground (Jdg. 13:19–20)

Much of God's appearing in the Bible takes place within one particular setting—the temple or sanctuary. "Do this," Moses says to the Israelites once the desert sanctuary has been set up, "and the glory of the LORD will be seen by you" (Lev. 9:6). Indeed, biblical texts consistently refer to the temple as the place where pilgrims will "see God's face."* But what could they actually *see* if there were no images of God in the temple?

Recently, scholars have focused on a few other peoples of the ancient Near East—there are not many—who also seem to have practiced a form of aniconism (avoidance of divine images) in

* This expression was apparently an idiom for appearing at a cultic site. It has been obscured by the long-standing practice of later generations to read the text as if it said, "You [Israelites] will be seen," rather than, "You will see" God, but this appears to be a later attempt to avoid the implications of this idiom, namely, that God can in fact be seen.

cultic settings. Sometimes what they did took the form of *empty-space aniconism:* a throne or platform was created for the god, but it was left empty—the god was, as it were, invited to come and occupy a space specially designated for him. Elsewhere, an object—a simple pillar or standing stone—would be walked around by the worshipers. The stone was not deemed an image of the god, although it could support him or represent his presence. This was how the ancient Nabateans, an Arablike people, worshiped. Their god (Dusares) was generally represented in nonfigurative betyls and stelae, but sometimes the Nabateans also made slightly iconic figures that represented the deity's eyes but nothing more. In Egypt existed a rather different concept of aniconic worship. There was a brief, twenty-year period during which Egyptian religion was programmatically aniconic (the period of the Amarna theology): no images were worshiped. But even outside of that period are elements suggestive of a kind of aniconism. The god Amun Re, state god of Egypt during the New Kingdom, was thus said to have no established image, and was invisible even to other deities: "None of the gods," says an Amun hymn, "knows his true form."

Thinking about biblical Israel in this broader context may be illuminating. Certainly, it should be clear by now that the Bible's prohibition of image making did not derive from any notion that God had no physical form—the God of Old, numerous texts imply, did indeed have some kind of physical being. But how that physicality was conceived—or *experienced*, one might say—is no doubt closely related to the whole subject of divine images that we have been pursuing. In fact, what the Bible says about the way that God was conceived to be present in the desert tabernacle or, later, in the temple is rather reminiscent of the empty-space aniconism just described. That is to say, the Israelites were commanded to set off a special space for God's presence in the innermost part of the sanctuary, the Holy of Holies. This sacred chamber was to contain a box (or ark) of acacia wood, overlaid with gold and topped with a golden cover. On each side stood a cherub—not like the baby cherubs of Renaissance paintings, but apparently carved statues of some sort of large, winged figure, perhaps with an animal body (though this is not clear):

> The cherubim will have their wings outstretched above. They will thus overspread the ark-cover with their wings, while their faces will be turned toward one another; toward the ark-cover will the faces of the cherubim be set [from either side]. . . . That is where I [God] will meet with you [Moses]. There, above the ark-cover, between the two cherubim that are on top of the ark of the covenant, I will speak with you of whatever I have to command you concerning the people of Israel. (Ex. 25:20, 22)

In other words, the wings of the cherubim, outstretched from either side above the ark, will constitute the bottom of a sacred zone (or throne, one might say), the very spot set off for God's presence. He will not be present there in a statue; He will not exist inside any form. But He will be there, or will be able to be there, in the empty space above the outstretched wings of the cherubim. Indeed, "The one who presides atop the cherubim" became a biblical way of referring to God (1 Sam. 4:4; 2 Sam. 6:2; 2 Kings 19:15; Isa. 37:16; Ps. 80:1, 99:1; 1 Chr. 13:6).

What is the message of such empty-space aniconism? It is tempting to associate this practice with Israel's distinctness (if not uniqueness) among the peoples of ancient Canaan. Israel's God *was* different, altogether different, from the gods of Canaanite cities or of Mesopotamia, as the Bible never tires of asserting. He was not to be represented in an image, *not* because He did not have a body, however, and not because He could not be seen by people. On the contrary: perhaps making an image of Him was forbidden precisely because the fact of His *appearing* among human beings, His being revealed, was (as we have seen) such a crucial item. He was a different kind of God. So there were to be no cultic statues; there was only an empty space, a designated area. There God could appear and be "seen" in a privileged moment, but not through an image, not in anything solid.

A further connection suggests itself between this idea and the examination of the moment of confusion two chapters previously. For there we glimpsed a God who can be, and was, seen, but was apparently not seen with what we might call normal sight. That is what the confusion was all about: at first He looks like a man, or a burning bush, or a fire, or something else—and then that first image fades and it becomes clear that it is God. Or to put it another way (perhaps, I admit, a bit tendentiously), the world of this God is not really the world that our eyes pick up, although it starts off by seeming to be that world.

In this context, the biblical insistence on not making images of this God, and the total absence of anthropomorphic representations of Him in the excavated cultic sites, seem particularly significant. What are these things saying, if not that this God will not inhabit a steady, visible image? You will not get Him into one of those statues; He may be conceived to have a body, but it is not a consistent presence. So the best we can do is designate a special space for Him to appear in, *a space that looks empty to the ordi-*

nary observer. Making an image of a god, we have seen, was not the act of a simpleminded savage: it was a way of inviting the god to inhabit the image's hands and feet and head. But such was emphatically *not* the way of this God; there was something about the steady, visible object that fundamentally contradicted the way that this God was "seen" when He was, the way He faded in. Wasn't that the real reason why making images of Him was forbidden?

5
The Cry of the Victim

One of the laws of Exodus provides a somewhat chilling glimpse at the workings of divine justice:

> And do not take advantage of the stranger or oppress him, for you [Israelites] were strangers in the land of Egypt. Do not abuse any widow or orphan. Because if you should abuse them, then they will certainly cry out to Me, and I will just as certainly hear them. Then I will become angry and kill you with the sword, so that your wives will become widows and your children orphans. (Ex. 22:21–24)

The common element shared by the stranger, the widow, and the orphan is their relative helplessness in society. Strangers (that is, resident aliens) were particularly easy to cheat or expropriate, since they lacked the usual entrenched network of clans and families that ordinary Israelites had. Numerous biblical passages therefore exhort Israelites to refrain from abusing or oppressing them (see Ex. 23:9; Lev. 19:10, 33–34, 23:22; Deut. 10:19, 14:29). In some of these passages one finds the same specific comparison found in the above passage: you were strangers in Egypt and did not like the way you were treated there, so do not mistreat the strangers among you now. As for widows and orphans, they also lacked the normal protection otherwise assumed for every Israelite. Specifically, the protection they lacked was that of the husband or father, who had all the rights in Israelite society and most of the power. Without him around to help them, his dependents were apparently easy prey. Other Israelites might have been tempted to take advantage of them, and so the law prohibited any such mistreatment.

It is interesting, however, that the prohibition and the punishment for its violation are not quite contiguous: the text does not say, "Do not do this, and if you should do it, then this will be your punishment." Instead, an intermediate element is evoked. If you abuse people who are in this weak, exposed position, "then they will certainly cry out to Me, and I will just as certainly hear them." It is the oppressed human's cry, in other words, that will unleash the chain of events that will ultimately result in your being punished. I am powerless *not* to react, God seems to say, once the abused party cries out to Me. This cry is worth considering, because it implies something about God that is at odds with our own beliefs.

ɞ ɞ ɞ

One ought to note in passing that the law does not exactly relate to the two parties equally. It is addressed to the potential oppressor: If *you* do this, then *he* will cry out, and I will have to act. It goes without saying that this was not the only way that the law could have been phrased. It might have been written entirely in the third person: "If a man abuses a widow or an orphan . . . ," or, "He who abuses . . ." This would have kept both parties at the same distance. The text might even have adopted the victim's standpoint: "If you are a widow or an orphan and someone abuses you . . ." But no; the oppressed party here is the *other* (just as the stranger was in the preceding law), whereas *you* are the one close to Me, the one to whom I am speaking. Nevertheless, I am telling you, my interlocutor, that there are limits to what you can do: if you victimize someone, then that someone will cry out and I will have to act against you.

The human cry is not a constant feature of divine–human interaction in the Bible; it seems to be connected specifically with the powerless. Interestingly, it occurs again just a few verses later in the book of Exodus.

> If you should take your fellow's garment in pledge [for a loan], you must give it back to him before the sun sets. After all, it is his only clothing, all that he has to cover his bare skin—what else can he sleep in? Consequently, if he cries out to Me, I will hear him, for I am compassionate. (Ex. 22:26–27)

Loans throughout most of the biblical period were basically a form of charity. A person was not to demand interest on a loan or to discount it (as the verse just preceding those cited states); money was lent to one's countrymen for free, mostly to poor farmers who needed something to tide them over until the harvest. But what if the farmer refused to (or could not) pay? The usual practice in loaning money was to secure the loan with a pledge: that is, the borrower would temporarily give the lender some valued possession that would be returned to him only when the loan was repaid. This was a standard demand and absolutely acceptable in most cases. But in the above passage, it is understood that the borrower is extremely poor: he has nothing of value to give, no prized bit of jewelry or family heirloom—only the shirt off his back. So that is what he offers. In such a case (similar to someone giving a millstone in pledge—Deut. 24:6), the lender is not to accept the pledged item, or at least he must return it before sunset, since keeping it would be grossly unfair. The text then goes on to explain this edict: obviously, this is the borrower's only real clothing; he would not be pledging such a valuable and vital item if he had another garment back home (that is, if the borrower owned *two* garments, he probably owned a lot of other things of lesser value as well, any one of which might now be pledged). But since it is his only real possession, then depriving him of it would be truly cruel—what could he sleep in during the cold night? After the text has mentioned all these things, one would think that there was nothing more to be said. Of course the lender should not keep such a pledge! And yet the text does not stop there but mentions one further consideration, the crucial element that will, once again, surely unleash a divine reaction: "If he cries out to Me, I will hear him, for I am compassionate."

When one stops to consider it, this cry of the victim actually appears to be somewhat problematic—and in more than one respect. First, its very mention seems to deny God's absolute knowledge of, and mastery over, His own world. The text implies that God does not, or does not always, know what is going on; sometimes the victim's crying out is required for God to be informed that oppression is taking place. The only alternative to this conclusion is at least equally troubling, namely, that injustice itself is of less vital concern to God than the pitiful human reaction it produces. He is disturbed principally by the cry and not the injustice that causes it. In the light of this problem, it is to be noted that a synthetic restatement in Deuteronomy of two of the laws seen above omits any mention of the victim's cry:

> Do not subvert the rights of the stranger [or] the orphan. Do not take a widow's clothing as a pledge. Remember that you were a slave in Egypt and the LORD your God redeemed you from there. That is why I am telling you today to observe this commandment. (Deut. 24:17)

This text does not content itself with merely alluding to the substance of the previously promulgated laws; it also mentions the justification seen earlier, the period of the Israelites' enslavement in Egypt. Yet somehow the victim's cry, prominent in the case of both the widow and the orphan and the pledged garment in the book of Exodus, is omitted here.

Beyond the theological problems implied by the victim's cry, the cry is perplexing for another reason—the fact (mentioned earlier) that these laws are addressed to the potential oppressor. It is not that this form of address is troubling in itself—why not warn potential offenders? But in presenting God as speaking directly to the oppressor about the victim's cry, the Bible makes Him seem almost like a well-disposed but powerless bureaucrat, shrugging His shoulders as He talks to the victimizer: "Normally, I'd be able to help you out, pal, but there's this matter of the oppressed person's cry. When that's there, there is nothing I can do but react." Why not simply say: "If you do this terrible thing, I will punish you with all the force of heaven"?

Precisely because of the problems it raises, the victim's cry might well have been omitted entirely from the Bible (as it was from the Deuteronomy passage cited). Why mention it at all? Yet it is mentioned, here and elsewhere. And so, once again, it might seem that the text is telling us something about its own world, something more than the actual subject that it is discussing.

ɞ ɞ ɞ

Part of the explanation might seem to lie with a minor bit of biblical physics, one that is often ignored even by scholars. In the biblical world sound was thought to travel upward. God, situated in heaven, was thus privy to whatever sounds might be made on earth, even if He could not necessarily see from such heights everything that was happening down below. How else might one explain God's words with regard to the sinful cities of Sodom and Gomorrah?

> And the LORD said, "The outcry of Sodom and Gomorrah is so great, and their sin is so very grievous! I will go down and see if they have indeed gone astray as their cry [indicates], and if not, then I will find that out. (Gen. 18:20–21)

According to the plain sense of this passage, the outcry arising from Sodom and Gomorrah has reached God in highest heaven. Nevertheless, He is apparently not entirely sure what is going on, which is why He proposes to "go down and see." Now, the text does not say that the outcry that reaches God is that of victims.

Given the rest of the story, one might be justified in thinking that what He heard was the sound of unbridled revelry and wanton merriment. In any case, if sound rises, this might go part of the way to explaining why the two laws examined earlier specifically mention the victim's cry—were not the sounds rising up from earth the normal way for God to find out about what was happening down here?

The notion is hardly far-fetched (though it is certainly some distance from the assertion of later theologians that God simply *knows*, that is, He is omniscient). Other peoples represented the gods as hearing sounds rising to heaven—in fact, in the ancient Mesopotamian *Atra-ḫasīs Epic* the gods resolve to destroy the world because the noise that human beings are making below is so great, and reaching them in heaven so clearly, that they are unable to sleep:

> The land became great, the peo[ple mu]ltiplied;
> the land became sated [?] like cattle.
> The god [Enlil] became disturbed [by] their
> gatherings.
> [The go]d heard their noise.
> He said to the great gods:
> "Great has become the noise of mankind;
> With their tumult they make sleep impossible."
> (*Atra-ḫasīs* [Babylonian], fragment 1, column
> 1, 2–8)

To the west as well, ancient peoples believed that sound rises, and Virgil even describes a great birdlike creature, Rumor (*Fama*), who "towers in the air" and whose attentive ears never miss tales, true or false, emanating from the humans below (*Aeneid* 4:173–90). Actually, this is somewhat reminiscent of Ecclesiastes' advice to ordinary mortals: "Do not curse the king even among your acquaintances, and do not curse a rich man even in your bedroom. For a *bird of the air* will carry the sound, and a winged creature may tell of the matter" (Eccles. 10:20).

But if sound was deemed to rise up to heaven or to be carried through the air by birds, that still will not explain the cry of the victim in the Bible. For what God is said to *hear* in the Bible is almost exclusively a cry of distress, or what is called in Hebrew a *ṣeʿaqah* (or sometimes the similar *zaʿaqah*). These words almost never refer to an ordinary yell or to the hubbub of many voices. Indeed, it may well be that even in the passage cited above concerning Sodom, the cry that God hears is not one of revelry at all, but of alarm or suffering. This was certainly how it was interpreted by some of the Bible's most ancient interpreters. Lacking a ready source for this (as they interpreted it) cry of distress, they created one. It came, they said, from a daughter of Lot (Abraham's nephew), whose kindness to strangers was discovered and punished by the Sodomites.

> Pelotit was Lot's daughter and she was married to one of the leaders of Sodom. She saw a poor man afflicted in the public square and she was sorely grieved for him. What did she do? Every day, when she went to draw water, she would take some food from her house and put it in her pitcher, and so would feed the poor man. When they found out, they took [the woman] to be burned. (*Pirqei deR. Eliʿezer* 25; also *Targum Pseudo-Jonathan* on Gen. 18:21)

Thus it was not just any human sound, but the piteous outcry of the righteous Pelotit that God heard arising from Sodom—in other words, it was this cry of the victim that caused Him to act. Now, the fact that these ancient interpreters rewrote the Genesis account to include this detail only demonstrates that they had well grasped the biblical cliché. For in the Bible, time and time again, what God hears is the *ṣeʿaqah* of the oppressed. Here, for example, is what God says to Moses in their first encounter at Mount Horeb:

> "I have indeed seen the suffering of My people who are in Egypt, and I have heard their cry *(ṣeʿaqah)* at the hands of their taskmasters; indeed, I know full well their plight. So I have come down to save them from the Egyptians and bring them back up from that land to a rich and spacious land, a land flowing with milk and honey—to the place of the Canaanite and the Hittite and the Amorite and the Perizzite and the Hivite and the Jebusite. But now, listen! The cry *(ṣeʿaqah)* of the Israelites is coming to me; indeed, I have seen the misfortune which the Egyptians are inflicting upon them." (Ex. 3:7–9)

This passage makes it amply clear that sound was not simply the means by which news of the Israelites' mistreatment reached God—after all, He also says that He has *seen* their suffering. But it is their piteous cry, their *ṣeʿaqah,* that makes that suffering unbearable to Him—He must act. And so it is elsewhere in the Bible:

> And the people denounced Moses, saying, "There is nothing to drink!" So he cried out *(ṣaʿaq)* to the LORD, and the LORD showed him a piece of wood. (Ex. 15:24–25)

The God of Old

"We cried to the LORD, the God of our fathers, and He listened to us and saw our suffering, our plight, and our misfortune. The LORD freed us from Egypt." (Deut. 26:7–8; similarly, Num. 20:16)

"When you cried out to Me, I saved you from them." (Jdg. 10:12)

When they cry out to the LORD against their oppressors, He will send a savior and a leader to save them. (Isa. 19:20)

Because of the groans of the plundered poor and needy, "I will now act," says the LORD. "I will give help," He affirms to him. (Ps. 12:5)

When people cry out the LORD hears and saves them from all their troubles. (Ps. 34:17)

Let the prisoner's cry reach You; free those who are condemned to death, as befits your power. (Ps. 79:11)

O LORD, God of my salvation, I cry out by day and by night before You,
Let my prayer reach You, turn Your ear to my cry.
For I am filled with troubles, I am at the edge of Sheol. (Ps. 88:1–3)

For He looks down from His holy heights: the LORD stares down from heaven to earth.
To hear the prisoner's cry and set free those who are condemned to death. (Ps. 102:19–20)

The LORD is near to all who call Him, to all who call to Him sincerely.

He fulfills the wishes of those who fear Him; He hears their cry and saves them. (Ps. 145:18–19)

He lets the cry of the poor come before Him, He heeds the cry of the needy. (Job. 34:28)

When You put them [the Israelites] in the power of their enemies and they oppressed them, they cried out to You in their time of trouble and You heard them from the heavens and in Your great mercy sent them a savior to save them from their enemies. (Neh. 9:27)

Although *ṣaʿaq* does mean "cry out," one might be tempted to understand it as simply a vivid way of referring to prayer in general. If so, are not the above passages really intended only to indicate that God hears all human beings when they pray? Such a message might be inferred from one or two of the passages, especially those cited from Psalms 34 and 145 (both of them, perhaps not coincidentally, assigned by most scholars to the end of the biblical period). Yet there certainly are other words and expressions that mean "to pray" in biblical Hebrew—"call out," "entreat," "commune," "lift up the hands," "fall down [in supplication]," and others. The above passages (and many more not cited) are not claiming that God heeds human prayers *in general;* the famous request of a torch singer, "O Lord, won't you buy me a Mercedes-Benz?" would not be covered by their theology. What these passages say is that God is uniquely moved by human suffering. This claim is made despite its theological difficulties—for, as pointed out earlier, God ought rightly to be aware of everything going on in His universe and not just the cry of the victim: moreover, the victim's cry ought hardly to be evoked when admonishing the potential victimizer. Despite such difficulties, this cry of the victim is hardly an obscure or minor part of the very conceptualization of divine-human interaction in the Bible—it is, par excellence, the thing that humans do that makes God act. Thus (to give but one more example), there is a line repeated again and again as a kind of refrain in Psalm 107, a survey of Israelite history. What are these words that constitute, in the psalmist's eyes, a leitmotiv in every age of Israel's history? "They cried out to the LORD in their adversity, and He saved them from all their troubles." But why?

6 6 6

An answer of sorts may be glimpsed in what is certainly one of the oddest psalms in the whole Bible.

> God stands in the divine assembly, among the
> gods He passes judgment:
> "How long will you [gods] judge falsely, showing
> favor to the guilty party?
> Give justice to the poor, the orphan; find in favor
> of the needy, the wretched.
> Save the poor and the lowly, rescue them from the
> wicked."
> (But they do not know or understand, they walk
> about in darkness; the earth's foundations are
> tottering.)
> "I used to think you all were gods and sons of the
> Most High;

yet you will die like humans, and fall like one of
those falling stars."
Arise, O God, judge the earth, since all the nations
now are Yours.

(Psalm 82)

This psalm actually addresses a set of problems that must have sorely vexed ancient Israelites. Why should there be only one God—and ours, at that!—when there are so many different nations in the world? Should not each nation have its own god or gods (as indeed most other nations believed was the case)? And if the answer is that these other nations' gods are abominations and utterly false, then why does the one true God allow them to exist? Should He not destroy their images and priests and temples—and at the same time stop being "our" God, and rule over all peoples equally?

Different answers to these questions were given in biblical times. The book of Deuteronomy seems to suggest in one or two places that these others gods, while inferior, do indeed have some power and perform a necessary function:

> [Moses tells the people:] Do not lift your eyes to the sky to see the sun and the moon and the stars, the whole host of heaven, and then turn aside and start bowing down and worshiping these, *whom the LORD your God has allotted to all the [other] peoples under the whole sky.* But you are the ones whom He took and brought out of the iron smelting pot of Egypt, to be His own property to this day. (Deut. 4:19–20)

The God of Old

When the Most High divided up mankind,
apportioning out the nations,
He established the borders of peoples to
correspond to the number of the sons of the
gods.
But the LORD's own portion is His people, Jacob is
His allotted property.

(Deut. 32:8–9)

According to both these texts, God Himself is responsible for the other gods: He assigned other nations to their care. However, He kept Israel for Himself rather than assigning it to some lesser denizen of heaven: they are His own "allotted property" (a term usually used for a person's inherited patch of real estate).

Psalm 82 presents a different understanding. It describes a scene in highest heaven that must have taken place long ago, even from the psalmist's perspective, a time when the skies were still full of active, efficacious gods. The scene itself is set in what the text calls the *'adat 'el* (translated above as "divine assembly"). Now, *'adat 'el* is a phrase with a history. It appears in slightly different form as *'adat 'ilm* in the library of inscribed clay tablets unearthed at ancient Ugarit (see previous chapter). In Ugaritic, as we have seen, the word El (sometimes a term for God in biblical Hebrew) was the name of a specific deity, the head of the Ugaritic pantheon. The phrase *'adat 'ilm* (as well as *puḫru 'ilm*) thus refers in Ugaritic to the great council of Canaanite gods over which El presides. Whether Psalm 82 is consciously adopting a concept from Ugarit or is simply invoking an idea that was part of the intellectual landscape of ancient Israel is difficult to determine. In any case, what Psalm 82 is saying is that, sometime long ago, God (here meaning the God of Israel) stood up in the *'adat 'el,* the council of the gods, and fired everyone. The reason He did so was that they were not doing their job competently—specifically, they were failing in what the psalm seems to hold is the most important area of a deity's functioning:

> "How long will you [gods] judge falsely, showing
> favor to the guilty party?
> Give justice to the poor, the orphan; find in favor
> of the needy, the wretched.
> Save the poor and the lowly, rescue them from the
> wicked."

Because the gods had failed to administer justice properly—it might not be wrong here to say that they had failed, in biblical terms, to hear the victim's cry—they were no longer fit to be gods. It is not clear from the context whether the parenthetical remark that follows the above-cited lines—namely, "But they do not know or understand, they walk about in darkness; the earth's foundations are tottering"—refers to the poor and the needy or to the gods who fail to give them the justice they deserve. I believe that the latter is correct, but it really does not matter; what the psalm is saying in any case is that, because the poor and the needy are being denied their due, the very existence of life on earth is being threatened, "the earth's foundations are tottering." Faced with such a situation, God must act. Even though the gods were created to be heavenly immortals, their apparent immortality is now to come to an end. Everyone has seen a shooting star, and the phenomenon of course fascinated and troubled ancient peoples; no doubt in earliest times it was thought to be the fall of a god from heaven. Psalm 82, it should be noticed, does not quite say this. It says that although they were created to be immortals, the other gods will fall from their heavenly perch *like* a falling star. But the result will be that only one deity, the God of Israel, will be left. All this, the psalm says, happened long ago, in days of yore. But if so, it concludes, then there is now no other force in heaven to oppose God, and all peoples are under His power, "since all the nations now are Yours." Therefore, the psalmist says, You ought to take up our cause, since You are unopposed.

Such is the message of this psalm, but we ought not to lose sight of our particular focus. It says that hearing the victim's cry is a god's duty, and God's duty. It says that if that job is not properly performed, the very foundations of the earth will shake. Most remarkably, it says this *not* because the psalm itself is a request for God now to take up the cause of the poor and downtrodden. This is no plea for social justice—that is not the psalm's apparent purpose. The fact that the gods were fired for failing to act in the interests of the poor is only so much background, a way of urging God to "arise" now and do something—presumably, save Israel—*because He is in charge of all nations*. It is, of course, possible to say that this psalm means to imply that Israel is collectively poor and downtrodden and in need of divine aid; that may indeed be the psalm's starting supposition, but it is in any case irrelevant. For the point is that, in order to get God to act, the psalmist recounts this scene in the council of the gods, a scene that simply assumes what everyone should know, that it is a god's duty to take care of the oppressed, and that it was the other gods' failure to perform this duty (and not some other duty, such as bringing the rain or causing the flocks to multiply or bringing about victory in war) that most plausibly explains why they were fired, leaving only God in charge.

It is this same assumption that seems to underlie the numerous references to the cry of the victim that we have seen. For surely, what we have seen is virtually a biblical reflex, a cliché that appears throughout the biblical period. It is just in the nature of things that victims will cry out to God and that God will hear them and act on their behalf—indeed, as Psalm 82 implies, the same thing was expected (or ought to have been) of any god in ancient times.

ꟹ ꟹ ꟹ

Was it—is it—in fact the nature of God to hear the victim's cry? Surely our own age is one in which such a claim is difficult to maintain. Our ears still ring with the terrified screams that rose up from the gas chambers, and to that massive human tragedy are added in each new decade the cries of thousands more, sometimes hundreds of thousands, innocent victims all. It is certainly difficult in this age to maintain that the sovereign of the universe always hears, or responds to, the victim's cry.

But if our age has witnessed innocent suffering on an unprecedented scale, we should not forget that ancient peoples were no less exposed to innocent suffering in regular, and sometimes massive, doses. To begin with, they lived in a world where something like one out of every two newborn children failed to reach its fifth birthday. "Why did the baby die?" must have been a question asked in virtually every family, and one that had no obvious answer. After all, a newborn child is innocent by definition; certainly the baby was not to blame. Was its death God's way of punishing the parents? But even if that could explain it, what did *they* do? Could there be so many guilty parents in so many different families? Surely when the baby first took sick, the mother and the father cried out piteously and begged God to heal the illness—why did He not hear the victim's cry then if, as the Bible seems to maintain axiomatically, it is His nature so to do? Tragedies such as this, reenacted with stunning predictability year in and year out, ought to have kept sensitivity to the victim's cry out of any biblical description of God's nature. How could it be true?

But beyond such local disasters were national ones. Plagues, earthquakes, and similar catastrophes were certainly known in the biblical world—the Bible does not fail to mention them, in fact. Did not the innocent victims of such disasters cry out to God? Warfare in the ancient Near East was gruesome almost beyond description. Under relatively favorable circumstances, a conquered people might merely be turned into the chain gangs or house servants of their conquerors, their wives and daughters dragged away from them to serve as prostitutes or concubines or ordinary slaves until they outlived their usefulness. Under less favorable circumstances, the defeated people would simply be slaughtered—sometimes slowly, during the long process of conquest itself, or sometimes all at once and in a large group, after the enemy forces had broken down the city gates. Did God hear those victims crying out? The book of Lamentations vividly records the sufferings of the Jews at the hands of the Babylonians as they tightened their long siege of Jerusalem:

> My eyes have no more tears and my insides are
> like clay.
> My feelings are numb at my people's catastrophe,

The Cry of the Victim

As little babies, infants, lie helpless in the streets.
They whine to their mothers, "I'm hungry!"
"Something to drink!"
But they're left like the helpless corpses in the
streets,
Although they languish in their mothers' arms.

Even jackals offer the breast to suckle their
young,
But not my people; they have turned crueler than
an ostrich in the desert.
A baby's tongue is stuck to the roof of its mouth
from thirst,
And little children beg for bread, but no one gives
them a crumb.
People who once fed on dainties are wasting in the
streets,
And those who went about in purple now sift
garbage.
This nation's sin must be greater than Sodom's,
Which was crushed in a flash, untouched by
human hands.
Her [Jerusalem's] rulers were purer than snow and
whiter than milk,
With limbs that were ruddy as coral and frames of
sapphire.
Now they are blacker than soot, unrecognized in
the streets;
Their skin lies shriveled on their bones, dried up
like wood. . . .

> Tenderhearted women boiled their children with
> their own hands.
> Then they ate them as food. This is my people's
> catastrophe.
>
> (Lam. 2:11–12, 4:3–8, 10)

All this is to say that, even if they were spared the spectacle of concentration camps and crematoria, ancient Israelites were hardly unfamiliar with the phenomenon of innocent suffering; indeed, it was probably more of a daily reality in their lives than in ours. So how could their belief in the cry of the victim survive the reality check of their daily life—how could this biblical cliché continue in the face of such contradictory evidence?

In asking this question, I am not asking the theologian's usual problem-of-evil question: how can an all-powerful deity permit injustice to triumph or evil to befall the righteous or innocent? Mine is a more lowly, and local, question—almost, one might say, a literary or even stylistic one: why keep bringing it up? After all, the world is what it is. Why should biblical texts keep saying that it is so different from what it appears to be—that, in the case at hand, God hears the cry of the victim, when so often He apparently does not? Certainly it would have been possible, within the framework of ancient Israelite religion, to maintain the opposite and say that this all-powerful God is quite inscrutable. Sometimes He listens, sometimes He doesn't. There would scarcely be any less reason to worship Him and seek His favor—and of course, such a view of God would seem to better fit everyday reality. Or if that path was, for some unknown reason, unacceptable, then why not simply pass over the issue of innocent suffering in silence—why keep coming back to the cry of the victim when it was only a potential source of embarrassment? The answer, it seems to me, must be that it was not a source of embarrassment. Somehow, the everyday world did not flash "Disconnect" when the subject of the victim's cry came up. Exactly why or how is far from clear, but certainly the fact itself is worthy of consideration.

ꙮ ꙮ ꙮ

One of the passages with which we began highlights a further aspect of this same question. The law of the pledged garment in Exodus said:

> If you should take your fellow's garment in pledge [for a loan], you must give it back to him before the sun sets. After all, it is his only clothing, all that he has to cover his bare skin—what else can he sleep in? Consequently, if he cries out to Me, I will hear him, *for I am compassionate.* (Ex. 22:26–27)

The indicated words are actually as much of a cliché as is the cry of the victim. For in the Hebrew Bible, it is a frequent assertion—so frequent as to deserve the label axiomatic—that God is by nature compassionate *(ḥannun).* Indeed, this word, along with its frequent partner, "merciful" *(raḥum),* is specifically reserved for God alone: the two are never used of mere human beings in biblical Hebrew. They do, however, occur frequently in descriptions of God. He is, as noted, *axiomatically* compassionate; it is simply His nature so to be. Indeed, this is what it says in what is the most important use of this pair of adjectives in the Bible, the well-known passage in chapters 33–34 of Exodus. My interest is really only in the appearance of the words *ḥannun* and *raḥum* at the end of the passage, but I will begin by sketching out the broader context.

The passage comes on the heels of the Israelites' great sin during their desert wanderings after the exodus from Egypt. Believing that Moses has died at the top of Mount Sinai, they resolve to create a great golden calf as an object of worship. When Moses comes down from the mountain and discovers the calf, he destroys it and likewise shatters the stone tablets on which God had inscribed His laws; afterward he chastises the people. He then seeks God's assurance that, despite this sin, He will not now abandon the Israelites.

> Moses said to the LORD: "See now, You are telling me to take this people up [to Canaan], yet You have said nothing about who You will be sending with me—despite the fact that You did say, 'I have singled you out by name and you have gained My favor.' Now, if I have indeed gained Your favor, please let me know Your ways so that I may indeed know *You,* and in that way [continue to] win Your favor. After all, this nation is Your own people." He replied: "My Countenance [*or* My "emissaries"?] will be going along, but I will be leaving you." Moses answered: "If Your Countenance is not going to go, then do not even have us depart from here. But how will anyone know that I have gained Your favor, I and this people of Yours, unless You Yourself go with us? And in that way we will be distinguished, Your people and I, from any other people on the face of the earth." (Ex. 33:12–16)

Exactly what "My Countenance" means in this text is disputed; some translators render the word as "presence," but that hardly seems to make sense. (Some ancient interpreters seem to have understood it as a reference to an angel, the "angel of the Countenance.") In any case, the issue certainly seems to be whether God, who until this time has been headquartered at "the mountain of God" (Horeb, Sinai) in the wilderness, will now leave that place and go with His adopted people to their new homeland, Canaan. Quite naturally, Moses is concerned about this issue. He does not want to leave without the assurance that God will be going along—and after the golden calf incident, he is quite justified in fearing that God might want to stay where He is and just send something or someone else. That seems to be what "My Countenance" represents here, something less than God's full presence.

> The LORD said to Moses, "All right, I will grant even this request of yours, since you really have gained My favor and I know you by name." Then Moses said: "Show me, I beg, Your glory [physical being]." He said: "All My goodness I can cause to pass before you, and I can proclaim the name 'the LORD' before you. But I am compassionate [only] with whom I choose, and merciful [only] with whom I choose." [Moses remains silent.] He said: "You cannot see My face, for no one can see Me and live." [Moses still remains silent.] The LORD said, "All right, here is a place next to Me to stand, on this rock. While My glory passes by I will put you in the cleft of the rock and cover you with My hand until I have passed. Then, when I take My hand away, you can see Me from behind, but My face will still not have been seen." (Ex. 33:17–23)

This passage has a wonderfully rich history of interpretation. From late antiquity through the middle ages and beyond, its apparent attribution to God of a physical body that can be seen was a source of scandal, and philosophers and theologians ingeniously struggled to read it in nonphysical terms. Their explanations are sometimes of breathtaking originality, but one is still left to wonder why a text should present such a straightforward picture of physical interaction if its intent were so sublimely metaphysical. With the rise of modern biblical scholarship, an opposite movement took place: this passage became a parade example of an early (and "primitive") Israelite conception of its God, a physical being not much bigger in size than an ordinary human. The passage's purpose would thus be to say that, although most people do not glimpse Him and live to tell about it, God nevertheless exists in as concrete a fashion as you or I do. Indeed, to the rule that humans are not allowed to see Him Moses was, according to this passage, granted a partial exception. God allowed him to glimpse Him "from behind," and it is this fact that the narrative is out to convey, indeed to celebrate.

But while such a reading seems correct as far as it goes, there is still one thing in the above passage that needs to be explained. What is the sense of God's intermediate offer (the one that apparently falls short of what Moses has requested)? He says: "All My goodness I can cause to pass before you, and I can proclaim the name 'the LORD' before you. But I am compassionate [only] with whom I choose, and merciful [only] with whom I choose." What, first of all, does it mean for God to cause "all My goodness" to pass before Moses and to "proclaim the name 'the LORD' before you"? This would seem to be a reference to what happens next in the narrative, when Moses climbs back up Mount Sinai:

> And the LORD went down in a cloud and stood there with him. Then He proclaimed the name of the LORD. The LORD passed in front of him and proclaimed: "The LORD, the LORD! A God compassionate and merciful, slow to anger and of great kindness and faithfulness, keeping kindness for thousands, forgiving sin and transgression and misdeed. Yet He does not [always] utterly acquit, but may visit the sin of parents on their children and children's children, on the third and even fourth generations." And Moses hurried and bowed down to the ground in prostration. (Ex. 34:5–8)

Here God does indeed "proclaim the name 'the LORD' " in front of Moses, just as He said He would. Indeed, it would seem that this act was itself one of extraordinary beneficence (it was not just a friendly self-identification)—so perhaps it is this that God meant earlier when He said He would cause "all My goodness to pass before you"; this phrase also refers to God's proclaiming His own name. But there is one striking difference between what I called above God's intermediate offer and what occurs here. In the intermediate offer God had said He would proclaim His name and cause His goodness to pass before Moses, but "I am compassionate [only] with whom I choose, and merciful [only] with whom I choose." I have actually been a bit loose in this translation; I hope I have captured the right sense, but the text more literally says, "I am compassionate with whom I am compassionate and merciful with whom I am merciful." These are the very two concepts we have been discussing, *ḥannun* and *raḥum*. The intermediate offer would thus seem to be God's willingness to proclaim His name to Moses but *not* to say anything about whom He will be compassionate and merciful with.

(It should not escape the reader that this intermediate offer is precisely what I identified earlier as a far more reasonable alternative to claiming that God is compassionate and merciful—He could simply be held to be inscrutable: "I am compassionate with whom I am compassionate and merciful with whom I am merciful.") What finally does get said, on the other hand, goes beyond this. God not only proclaims His name to Moses but also says outright what He had previously said He would withhold—He asserts that He is by nature *ḥannun* and *raḥum,* compassionate and merciful. "I am compassionate with whom I am compassionate and merciful with whom I am merciful" may be all that God was willing to say before, but to Moses God now reveals the withheld truth.

Who is right about this passage—the medieval metaphysicians, or the modern biblical scholar? In the light of what was seen in the preceding chapters, I would be inclined to read this passage in a way somewhat different from both. God here is indeed presented as an altogether physical being, not much bigger, apparently, than Moses himself. And yet . . . there is something quite eerie and otherworldly about this confrontation. Notice, for example, the setting. God goes down to Mount Sinai to meet with Moses. The text is actually somewhat emphatic on this point: "And the LORD went down in a cloud and *stood there with him.** Then He proclaimed the name of the LORD. The LORD *passed in front of him* and proclaimed." In other words, God and Moses here are standing virtually face-to-face, as close

* This particular form of the verb actually means something more like "to take a stand," "to position onself"—and is different from simply "standing" *('md, nṣb)*; its use here is thus in itself somewhat emphatic.

as they could ever come (God's "body," however, is being shielded by a cloud, presumably to protect Moses from death). I hope I will not be going too far if I compare this moment to the various "foggy" confrontations with angels (that is, angels that turn out to be God Himself) seen in Chapter 2. What takes place, however, is not a revelation of the angel's true identity, but God's proclamation that He is by nature *ḥannun* and *raḥum,* compassionate and merciful, along with the other divine traits He then recites. One cannot escape the impression that this recitation is itself being presented as an act of self-revelation.

This biblical announcement of God's compassionate nature thus seems to be connected to some of the broader themes of perception and appearance that we have been examining. But before leaving this passage, I would like to add a last word about the sentence just mentioned, "The LORD *passed in front of him* and proclaimed. . . ." Again, the highlighted words have a rich history of interpretation—but what do they really mean in context? Surely God does not pass in front of Moses to be heard better or so that Moses can get a better look at the cloud. Instead, this phrase appears designed to mark some change, indeed, some changed *perception,* just as when God opened Balaam's eyes and he saw the angel, or when the other angels were first recognized by their human interlocutors. God passes in front of Moses and then, after that, something is different—so different that Moses reacts exactly as Joshua and Manoah and Abraham had in their confrontations with God when they suddenly understood who it was: Moses "hurried and bowed down to the ground in prostration." But Moses does not, apparently, *see* anything new—he hears God say that He is merciful, and he apparently stands closer to God than ever before. Now, what God actually says to

Moses about His being merciful is really not news—as we saw in Psalm 82, it was simply any god's job to be compassionate and merciful, and this truth was so universally assumed in the Bible that, as we have seen, it underlies the dozens of passages that speak of the victim's cry. Yet here, in Exodus, this cliché is presented as a revelation, God's ultimate self-revelation to Moses: I am by nature *ḥannun* and *raḥum* (despite all evidence to the contrary). I hear the cry of the victim; I can't help it.

6

The Soul's Journey

There is an old devotional poem found at the beginning of many Hebrew prayer books, including some printed today. Composed (according to the acrostic signature of its verses) by a certain Shemaʿyah, it tells of the doings of the soul late at night, in the dark hours before daybreak. The poem has always haunted me. Although it is not heard much anymore, it was originally composed to be sung by worshipers, and it was in such a form that I first came to know it. Its slow, minor-key melody gives the words a gravity they simply cannot have on the printed page.

Apart from the melody, however, duplicating the effect of the words themselves in English is quite a challenge. The reason is that this poem is written in the allusive style of medieval Hebrew, in which nearly every line is a patchwork of different biblical phrases. That is, the poet, although writing an original composition, incorporates into every line one or two phrases or expressions, or even a short sentence, from the Bible. (The poet can do this because he basically knows the whole Hebrew Bible by heart; in fact, he expects that you do too and so will recognize his borrowings.) The result is a kind of collage that is endlessly alluding to different biblical stories and psalms and prophecies, all the while pursuing its own, original course. Here, for example, are the opening words of the poem (which also functioned as a refrain at the end of each succeeding stanza when it was sung):

> *'Odeh la 'El lebab ḥoqer*
> *Beron yaḥad kokhebei boqer.*
> I will sing to God, who probes the heart,
> As all the morning stars give voice.

The phrase "who probes the heart" is meant to evoke the prophet Jeremiah's use of this phrase for God (Jer. 17:10), while the words "as all the morning stars give voice" come from a well-known verse in the book of Job (38:7). The two lines rhyme, of course *(ḥoqer . . . boqer),** and as rhymes often do, this one succeeds in connecting two things originally separate and making their conjunction feel appropriate, even inevitable. When is the right time to sing to Him who probes the heart? Why, when all the morning stars give voice. And this, of course, fits with the poem's intended setting: it was composed to be sung by those who gather for prayer in the very early hours of the day, when the sky is still black and dotted by the morning stars. Those stars, in Job's phrase, do not merely "give voice" or "sing"; they *rōn* (a Hebrew word whose sound, perhaps because of English, has always sug-

* In fact, every stanza in the poem ends with a biblical verse that contains the word "morning" *(boqer)*. Incidentally, the *q* here represents the Hebrew letter *qof,* pronounced like a *k* but at the very back of the mouth.

gested to me here a kind of polyphonic, electric droning, such as the stars might be making in the famous van Gogh painting). In any case, an ancient conceit (reflected in the Job verse but certainly older) had it that the stars that we see in the sky are in fact the visible manifestation of a choir of angels that continually sings God's praises on high. The poet thus proposes in these opening words that he and his fellow worshipers now join together, under the stars, in praising God along with this chorus of angels:

> I will sing to God, who probes the heart,
> As all the morning stars give voice.
>
> Think now of the soul, sparkling
> Like amber, agate, amethyst,
> Whose light is as bright as the sun,
> Seven times the light of morning.
>
> Hewn from the Glorious Throne,
> She [the soul] went to the land of Arabah—
> To be saved from the raging fire
> And made radiant before morning.
>
> *[To "you" in the plural:]*
> Awake now, for every night
> Your soul rises up on high
> To give reckoning for her deeds
> To the Maker of evening and morning.
>
> He finds her sullied and soiled
> From sins and all their ilk,
> Like a handmaiden betrothed,
> Morning after morning.

Faithful with what is lent [that is, with the soul],
God gives her back as He wills;
For no one perishes from sin,
"And it was evening and it was morning."

So keep this little one alive,
A pure soul, free of stain,
For he whose soul is not revived—
How will he live to see morning?

The content of the poem is easily summarized. The poet urges his fellow worshipers to consider their own souls, which he compares to the sparkling jewels on the high priest's breastplate, "amber, agate, amethyst." It is no accident that they sparkle so, he says: human souls are actually little pieces of God's own heavenly throne, but they have been chipped off and exiled to the world of mundane, everyday existence. Yet all is not lost. For the poet then goes on to describe how every soul travels at night back to its Maker in heaven, "to give reckoning for her deeds" and be cleansed from all the sins of the preceding day. This cleansing is crucial, for no matter how dirty the soul is when she arrives in the evening, God sends her on her way again pure and refreshed by morning.

To this heavenly journey of the soul I wish to return presently. My main interest, however, is a stylistic feature of the poem that is, I think, chiefly responsible for the haunting quality mentioned earlier. It is something I call *starkness,* a characteristic this poem shares not only with a good deal of religious poetry written after the Bible, but even with parts of the Bible itself. What is starkness? I must confess from the beginning that I do not have an exact definition but only a collection of impressions—impressions that I hope, as I assemble them, may give the reader some feeling for what I mean. To begin with, starkness is the very obvious unworldly quality found in this poem. The whole thing seems to take place in some sort of moonscape, altogether eerie and uncanny. Usual, ordinary existence—the realm of sunlight and daily life—is pointedly being contrasted here to another sort of being entirely, whose reality is overwhelming. The contrast is explicit: the little soul itself is "as bright as the sun," and the light it emits is (in words echoing Isa. 30:26) "seven times the light of morning." Everyday existence and *its* sun are just drab by comparison. Indeed, what we call the real world is almost entirely absent here: it is simply a desert waste, the place of "sins and all their ilk." This daylight realm may in any case be dismissed as secondary, since it is a mere carrying out, or reflection, of the significant events that take place on high in the world of the night. *That* world is quite overwhelming. Visited through the soul's journey, it opens onto the brilliant light of God's heavenly presence. This is the only reality that counts in this poem. Even the soul's human owner is not her real mate, since she has only been lent temporarily to the human being and is thus a sort of "handmaiden betrothed." By these words the poet seeks to evoke a certain law in the Bible (Lev. 19:20) while giving it a poetic twist.* The soul, he says, is indeed like an indentured handmaiden, living in her human owner's dwelling and forced to do all the housework and drudgery—and perhaps worse—that is a hand-

* In truth, the poet has inherited this metaphor from earlier poets and therefore has no need to explain the image.

maiden's lot; but she does not truly belong to him, since she is engaged to God and now yearns for her real Betrothed in heaven.

ɞ ɞ ɞ

This is certainly part of starkness. On the basis of this poem alone, one might be tempted to see starkness as essentially a medieval phenomenon, part of the medieval mystics' quest for divine union, which by definition led them out of this world and into another that was altogether uncanny. That may be true, but starkness did not begin in the middle ages. If the concept as a whole is not easily defined, the reality is in any case not difficult to spot—and it starts much earlier. Here is a brief glimpse of it in the book of Daniel:

> The mystery [of the king's dream] was revealed to Daniel in a nighttime vision. Then Daniel blessed the God of heaven. Daniel proclaimed: Let the name of God be blessed forever and ever, for wisdom and might belong to Him. He changes the times and seasons, removes kings and sets up kings, gives wisdom to the wise and knowledge to those who have understanding. He reveals deep and hidden things. He knows what is in the darkness and the light is with Him. To You, O God of my fathers, I give thanks and praise, since You have given me wisdom and might and now have made known to me what I requested of You; for You have informed me of the king's matter. (Dan. 2:19–23)

Here too we catch sight of a kind of moonscape, a place of bright light and deep shadows. That is, ordinary reality is full of "deep and hidden things" that only God may reveal; He "knows what is in the darkness and the light is with Him." The external world, the things one sees with one's eyes, certainly exists, but as in the song, it is completely downplayed: nothing significant happens there. Revolutions, the rise and fall of empires, are pointedly compared to the change of seasons in the year: they may seem for a time to be great upheavals, but they are merely part of a larger cycle of changes controlled by God. Kings and emperors are in fact mere pawns, "for wisdom and might belong to Him." In keeping with the moonscape, human beings, too, fall into categories that contrast as sharply as light and darkness: God "gives wisdom to the wise and knowledge to those who have understanding." The wise, here as elsewhere in the stark world, are a set class of human beings and an entirely static category; their opposites are the foolish, and there is nothing in between them. The two will never change and never meet.

૭ ૭ ૭

The opening psalm in the book of Psalms illustrates a second aspect of starkness, the absolute opposition between good and evil, righteousness and wickedness. There is no moonscape here—the images are drawn from the world of everyday sunlight—and yet, on closer inspection, there is something quite unworldly nonetheless.

> Happy the man who has not walked in the counsel
> of the wicked, nor stood on the path of sinners,
> nor sat in the gathering-place of fools.
> Instead, his desire is for the LORD's teaching, and
> he studies His teaching night and day.
> So he shall become like a tree rooted near a

> flowing stream: he will yield up fruit in its season,
> his leaf will not wither, and all that he does will
> prosper.
> Not so the wicked! They will be like chaff that the
> wind blows about.
> Thus, the wicked shall not withstand the
> judgment, nor shall sinners survive with the
> righteous.
> For the LORD takes care of the path of the
> righteous, but the path of the wicked shall perish.
>
> (Psalm 1)

The careful construction of this piece—it was apparently composed to be a kind of preface to the book of Psalms as a whole*—may elude a first-time reader. The righteous man, who is the subject of the three-part opening sentence of this psalm, is described as avoiding the company of a series of decreasingly serious offenders. In the first clause of this verse he is said to stay away from "wicked," and these are certainly meant to be understood as worse than the mere "sinners" whom he avoids in the second clause (in Hebrew this word for "sinner" still carries a note of inadvertency connected to its verbal root, which means "to miss the mark"). Less threatening even than the company of these sinners is that of the "fools" (or "scoffers") of the third clause, whose offense seems to be merely one of attitude rather than the actual commission of sin. Along with this catalogue of decreasingly serious offenders is a parallel progression of in-

* Compare Jer. 17:5–8.

creasingly passive involvement: the righteous man does not *walk* with the wicked, nor even *stand* with sinners, nor yet *sit* with fools—that is, he avoids even the most inactive activity with the least offensive of them.

However, the first question this psalm probably raises in the minds of most readers concerns not its construction but its message. Where am I in all this? one asks. Certainly I am not the wholly righteous fellow of the first verse. Some people may honestly be said to have shunned the wicked throughout their lives, but probably few even of these could claim to have avoided merely being present in the "gathering-place of fools" at any time in their existence. But if I am not this righteous fellow, then where do I belong? I don't feel like one of the wicked; for one thing, I don't think I am quite as intent on evil as "wicked" implies. I may be one of the sinners, but somehow it would seem unfair to sum up my existence with that one pathetic word. If truth be told, I suppose I have belonged to almost all these categories at different moments in my existence—sometimes, certainly, a fool, undeniably a sinner at other times, maybe even righteous for a moment or two. So why doesn't the psalm say something like that, something a little more realistic? Why evoke these merely theoretical categories, the altogether righteous and the unredeemably wicked, when most human beings we encounter seem to belong wholly to neither most of the time?

Yet it is precisely the sharp contrast between righteousness and wickedness that characterizes whole sections of the Bible—the book of Proverbs, for example. These, people are always either righteous or wicked (or the equivalent, seen in Daniel, "wise" or "foolish"). No middle ground is ever contemplated.

A righteous man's name is a blessing, but the name of wicked men rots. (Prov. 10:7)

What the wicked man fears he ends up with, but the wish of the righteous is granted. (10:24)

In the goodness of the righteous a city rejoices, and when the wicked disappear there is gladness. (11:10)

No harm befalls the righteous, but the wicked are full of misfortune. (12:21)

He who trusts in his wealth will fall, but the righteous like a leaf will flourish. (11:28)

The house of the wicked will be destroyed, but the tent of the upright will flourish. (14:11)

The heart of the wise seeks out knowledge, the mouth of fools pursues foolishness. (15:14)

Numerous psalms display the same mentality:

The wicked in his arrogance hounds the oppressed—may such people be caught in the very traps they have devised.
The wicked man is proud of what his greed has gotten him, and the profiteer curses God and scorns Him. (Ps. 10:2–3)

Give me justice, LORD, in keeping with my righteousness and innocence.
Let the wicked man's evil come to an end, and strengthen the righteous one . . .
God gives justice to the righteous and is wrathful [against the wicked] every day. (Ps. 7:8–9, 11)

> The LORD watches over all who are loyal to him, but all of the wicked He crushes. (Ps. 145:20)

> How long will the wicked, O LORD, how long will the wicked exult?
> How long will they speak so arrogantly, these evildoers who exalt themselves? (Ps. 94:3–4)

Certainly there is something conventional operating here: especially in those biblical writings known as wisdom literature (principally, the books of Proverbs, Job, and Ecclesiastes), the division of humanity into the categories of righteous and wicked seems almost automatic. But just because something is conventional or automatic does not mean it is not significant. As with the conventions that we saw in connection with the appearance of biblical angels, so here, too, there seems to be something important, even fundamental, underlying the convention. And so we should ask: what is it that could push biblical authors, generation after generation, to describe humanity in a way that seems so unrealistic, so disconnected from our own notion of ourselves and our experience of others? The answer, it seems to me, has to do with a certain mind-set, or way of seeing, in which all the normal shades and colors of our sunlight world are turned to a brilliant but unearthly brightness or to correspondingly dark shadows. I mean to say that starkness is less a matter of perceiving different things than of *perceiving the same things in a different way.* In this sense it may be related to the angel narratives examined in an earlier chapter. True, there is no *click* here, no sudden moment of recognition; but once again it is a matter of changed perception, of a world turned strange. Other people, after all, normally live out there in the sun world, the domain of everyday perception in which all their individuality—their quirks and freckles and favorite turns of phrase—are plain to see and hear. By contrast, the way of perceiving that underlies the verses cited (even if it eventually became a mere convention) is one in which human faces, along with everything else, turn stark. Everything particular or individual about people is abstracted into a single, stark judgment: wicked or righteous, foolish or wise.

I believe, incidentally, that it is no accident that *night* is sometimes evoked in these "stark" passages. It is the right moment for this kind of contemplation, in which the merely visible takes a backseat to another way of seeing, when right and wrong and the world of the soul emerge from the shadows. Here is a particularly telling passage from the book of Isaiah:

> At night I yearn for You with all my being, I seek
> You out with the spirit deep inside me.
> For when your judgments are [carried out] on
> earth, those who live in the world learn
> righteousness.
> If the wicked man is pardoned, righteousness is
> not learned; in the land of uprightness, he still
> does evil. He does not perceive God's splendor.
>
> (Isa. 26:9–10)

Here, in two verses, is the whole inventory of starkness: nighttime, the "spirit deep inside me," righteousness versus evil, and "God's splendor." Note the combination of nighttime and the soul's searching (or being searched) elsewhere:

Through the watches of the night my eyes stay
open. I am awake but do not speak.
My thoughts turn to days of old, to years gone by.
Let me say my prayer at night; let me commune
with my own heart and my spirit will be
searching.

(Ps. 77:4–6)

When Your judgment of me comes forth, may
Your eyes see that I am right.
You have visited me at night, searched my mind,
You have tested me and found nothing amiss.

(Ps. 17:2–3)

ɞ ɞ ɞ

None of this starkness seems particularly inviting. It is all so severe, absolute, black-and-white, whereas we normally live in a world bathed in warm sunlight. Flesh tones, and the touch of flesh, are what draw us on, along with all the other vivid details of our earthly existence. Starkness will have none of this. What is perhaps most forbidding about it is that it nonetheless purports to belong to *this* world, to describe people and events that really exist, but in terms that are quite foreign to our everyday way of being. People are turned into categories and all the usually important things of the world are pushed aside in favor of some eerie, remote, altogether spiritual reality. I suppose that is why there is a marked tendency to avoid the book of Proverbs and stark psalms such as those cited (a tendency found, perhaps surprisingly, even among biblical scholars). People naturally seem to gravitate to other kinds of writing within the Bible. But I think this is a mistake. Perhaps precisely because it is so different from our normal way of seeing, the stark way needs to be thought about seriously. What could push someone, what *did* push someone—many someones in fact—to see reality this way? And is it possible to re-create that state of mind?

There is another kind of starkness—but I think it is related—that is particularly characteristic of Moses' long speech that comprises our book of Deuteronomy.

> Behold, I set before you this day a blessing and a curse. The blessing, if you obey the commandments of the LORD your God, which I am commanding you today; and the curse, if you do not obey the commandments of the LORD your God, but turn from the path that I am commanding you today, and follow other gods who have not been your own. . . .
>
> Today you stand, all of you, before the LORD your God—your chiefs and leaders, elders and officials, every householder in Israel, plus your children, your wives, and the stranger in the midst of your camp, from woodcutter to water-carrier. . . . Behold, I have set before you today life and goodness, and death and evil. . . . I call heaven and earth today to witness concerning you: life and death am I setting before you, the blessing and the curse. Choose life, so that you may live, devoted to the LORD your God, obeying and clinging to Him. For He is your life and your survival, [allowing you] to dwell on the land which the LORD promised to give to your ancestors, to Abraham, to Isaac, and to Jacob. (Deut. 11:26–28; 29:10–11; 30:15, 19–20)

Here life itself consists of stark, absolute choices: blessing or curse, life or death, and nothing in between. One might ask here the same question as was asked of the righteous-versus-wicked, light-versus-darkness type of starkness: how often in our existence does it happen that things are so clear-cut? And even supposing the ancient Israelite who heard these words then made the stark choice and said yes to obeying the commandments, yes to life and the blessing—would the rest of his or her life continue in the same starkness, the all-or-nothing-ness of its presentation here? This is not life as most of us know it day by day, hour by hour: the details of our daily activities, the little errands, the endless conversations drive out the absolute. The starkness of the choice may be real, but it is far from our everyday reality, far from the world of the sun. But I would be remiss if I did not also note the element of starkness conveyed by the oft-repeated "today" of the above passage (and throughout the book of Deuteronomy). "Today" does not just designate the time or occasion. Here it is also an implied imperative: make up your mind, what'll it be? You don't have a lot of time.

The connection between this kind of starkness and the starkness of the righteous-versus-wicked hardly needs articulation; indeed, it is present in Psalm 1, examined above. There, as reward for his scrupulous eschewing of the wicked, the righteous man is promised that he

> shall become like a tree rooted near a flowing
> stream: he will yield up fruit in its season, his
> leaf will not wither, and all that he does will
> prosper.

> Not so the wicked! They will be like chaff that the wind blows about.
> Thus, the wicked shall not withstand the judgment, nor shall sinners survive with the righteous.
> For the LORD takes care of the path of the righteous, but the path of the wicked shall perish.

In other words, the one who, in Deuteronomy, makes his choice to obey God's commandments is the same as the righteous man here, whose "desire is for the LORD's teaching," and they share the same happy fate: a life of blessing and divine protection, utterly the opposite of the wicked man's fate.

ɞ ɞ ɞ

Anyone acquainted with European art and architecture in the middle ages will recognize that what I have called starkness has a great deal to do with medieval aesthetics—those paintings and sculptures that seem so little interested in what we would call the realistic portrayal of the human body, or that style of building in which the human dimension is lost in the great upward sweep of column and pointed arch and flying buttress. Certainly the connection between this stark way of seeing and the deep spirituality of Europe during this period is not accidental. It was a time when artists and architects sought to give expression to the inner life of the soul rather than depict the merely external and superficial features of the body, and a time when, as perhaps never before, human beings were aware of their utter smallness and frailty in the presence of their almighty Creator. Along with this came the stark polarizations: devils and angels, gold-haloed saints and their red-faced, hate-breathing opponents, the delights of paradise and the fiery netherworld of the utterly damned. But the middle ages seem almost as far away from us as the biblical period.

I find something oddly reminiscent of this same aesthetic a little closer at hand, in the vague feeling of disappointment that comes over me on those infrequent occasions when I go to a major league baseball game. What makes the experience of watching a baseball game on television so different from watching it at the stadium itself—and what does this difference mean? Of course, almost everyone prefers the real thing—being right there in the crowd, seeing the real players instead of dots on a screen, seeing the batter swing and, a split second later, hearing the crack of the real bat. These pleasures are undeniable—so who would not prefer being at the stadium to staying at home? Yet I must confess that whenever I actually do go to the ballpark, I always feel a certain letdown, one that comes with the realization that, after all, what I am watching is just a game. True, those athletes on the field are extraordinarily skillful, but at bottom they are an altogether recognizable item—I knew them, or people very much like them, when I was in high school. So here they are in front of me now, twenty or thirty years younger than me at this point (this does not add to their prestige in my eyes!), and seeing them as a group neatly spaced around the baseball diamond, with this player over here and that one over in back of him, I inevitably get a feeling for the whole scene: I am a spectator at a game being played between two groups of young men. What comes over the television screen, by contrast, is of an entirely different character. One has no sense of the group or even of the individual player: what one sees is a single great face that fills up the screen. This is the batter, and in his eyes one can glimpse a great deal of the *real* conflict in which he is engaged. He is hopeful and afraid, and perhaps, just now, also the slightest bit arrogant (or is that just bravado?), completely focused on one thing, the ball that is about to come shooting his way at incredible speed. Meanwhile the camera has switched to his opponent on the mound, and his face, too, now fills the screen: but he is patient, drawing on seasons of experience and, perhaps, a last-minute hunch to help him choose just the right pitch in just the right place, summoning his greatest powers from somewhere and pouring them all into one single, practiced motion. The conflict between these two is abstract, stark, yet on television it is laid out in a way that is altogether available and obvious; everyone can see it. Who wants any sense of the whole or any accurate portrayal of the human form when this is what the game is really all about? And so, all the rest melts away—for the moment, it is only these two souls that count.

Along the same lines, I have often thought that the great works of medieval spirituality—Dante's *Divine Comedy,* for example—could never be made into a movie. Somehow, Dante and Virgil would end up seeming like slightly comical heroes in some sort of oddly costumed buddy film, full of mopped brows and "whew's" as the pair steadily make their way to the end of purgatory. All the heraldry and gesture, the whole abstract, slow-motion pageantry of the poem, would dissipate the minute its words were represented by real human beings, with all their particulars, on the big screen.

But what about an animated cartoon? This might indeed work better, and it is interesting to consider why. To begin with, in cartoons there are no particulars. Everything is abstract, everything is in primary colors, without wrinkles or shadows. *There is no sunlight.* (Sometimes, of course, a cartoon will represent the sun, but then it is just a big yellow circle with hairlike rays shooting out or hanging listlessly at its side, and the shadows, if they are portrayed at all, are great black or purple blobs that chase the characters over the face of a distant hill. But everything the real sun brings—the texture and detail of everyday life—is, by definition, missing in a cartoon.) It is certainly no accident that the story line of the cartoon is equally stark: it is always the righteous mouse against the wicked cat, and the outcome is known in advance. Righteous Mouse will triumph (just as in the biblical proverbs cited above). How significant, then, that this world is what it is. In some ways it *looks* like the sun world; it has the same things—people and houses and trees and sky—but these all turn out to be different. Ordinary reality does not exist. For example, no one dies, ever. The characters (Righteous Mouse *or* Wicked Cat) always just dust themselves off after the most horrendous fall. Their bodies twist (like the prophet Jeremiah's in a certain medieval painting I know) into inhuman contortions of themselves as they are turned into living slingshots, stretched like chewing gum between two trees or wrapped four or five times around a flagpole—clearly, here is no taste for realism. The senses themselves are revealed to be altogether treacherous. The same trompe l'oeil by which a humanoid angel turns out to be God is regularly represented on the cartoon screen. Righteous Mouse draws a phony mouse–hole on the baseboard wall and, believing it to be real, Wicked Cat runs smashing into it face first as he chases his prey. Then, an instant later, Righteous Mouse himself is speeding toward it—oh no! But somehow, miraculously, the same phony hole turns out now to be real and the mouse disappears into it, he is saved—why or how is never explained, but righteousness must triumph, so it really does not matter.

One might ask why we like to depict such things when they are so contrary to our own experience of the world, and why, specifically, the stark primary colors of an animated cartoon are the preferred medium for their depiction. In the world of biblical starkness, I believe we have the beginnings of an answer, and it is similar to the answer offered by defenders of medieval aesthetics in the face of our modern taste for more realistic representation. This is a different kind of realism; it is talking about something that we may instinctively recognize even if it is far away from the everyday reality we are used to talking about, far from the world of the sun.

ʚ ʚ ʚ

Few people, when they think about it, will fail to recognize this starkness as a common element in religious perception. It is, as I said, hardly limited to the Hebrew Bible. Even those who do not know it firsthand from their own lives can see its reflection here and there in the world about: in those wonderful record album covers of gospel music, for example, with their dramatic, painted depictions of Little Man caught in a sudden yellow spotlight flashing through darkness; or in televangelists' programs with titles like *Hour of Decision, Hour of Power.* It is there for all to see in what is certainly one of the pieces of Protestant hymnody most widely known in America, "Amazing Grace":

> Amazing grace! (How sweet the sound!)
> That saved a wretch like me.

The Soul's Journey

I once was lost but now am found,
Was blind but now I see.

'Twas grace that taught my heart to fear
And grace my fears relieved.
How precious did that grace appear
The hour I first believed.

Through many dangers, toils, and snares
I have already come.
'Tis grace has brought me safe thus far,
And grace will lead me home.

The Lord has promised good to me,
His word my hope secures:
He will my shield and portion be
As long as life endures.

Yes, when this flesh and heart shall fail,
And mortal life shall cease,
I shall possess within the veil,
A life of joy and peace.

The earth shall soon dissolve like snow,
The sun forbear to shine,
But God, who call'd me here below,
Will be for ever mine.

I have printed the text as originally written by its author, John Newton, in the collection *Olney Hymns* (1779), but that text has been altered by subsequent editors and is probably known to most people today in slightly different form: many of the "I's" have become "we's" in today's version, and in place of the last two, or sometimes three, stanzas a single new one has been substituted:

> When we have been ten thousand years
> Bright shining as the sun,
> We've no less days to sing God's praise
> Than when we'd first begun.

What is *stark* about this hymn? One might better ask what is not. The subject is the speaker's total transformation: he goes from wretch to blessed soul, from lost to found, from blind to free. Here we are again in the world of absolute polarities, with no middle ground. Indeed, to say "in the world of" is to distort the whole character of this hymn: there is no world to speak of here, no outside, only the inner, spiritual reality of God's "amazing" (in today's English, "astounding," "inexplicable") gratuitous kindness, or what is called in biblical Hebrew *ḥesed*. This grace has brought the speaker to religious consciousness (" 'Twas grace that taught my heart to fear") while at the same time offering him comfort from ordinary terrors; its very arrival is presented as stark, operating on the same plane of imperative time as Deuteronomy's "today," that is, "the hour I first believed." As for the outside world, it is, when alluded to at all, altogether schematic and abstract—"mortal life," a place of "many troubles, toils, and snares." Beyond this it has no reality. It is certainly no accident that the sun—the embodiment of what we call the real world, the everyday reality we know—makes an appearance at the end of this hymn, but only in a negative sense:

> The earth shall soon dissolve like snow,
> The sun forbear to shine.

Nothing that is solid, nothing that we know through the world of the senses, is of any lasting significance; it can all simply melt away, leaving the true, spiritual reality alone. Although it is not part of the original hymn, the extra stanza cited above is altogether in keeping with the spirit of the rest, indeed starker still:

> When we have been ten thousand years
> Bright shining as the sun,
> We've no less days to sing God's praise
> Than when we'd first begun.

Here again is a world without sun; *we* are the sun, and even the laws of common sense do not hold. Ten thousand plus infinity equals infinity.

One might well ask if starkness is really as foreign to the everyday world as I have claimed. Are there not indeed such radical polarities, hours of decision, total transformations that actually occur in people's lives, from lost to found and from blind to seeing? The question is particularly apposite in the case of this hymn, whose author never tired of telling his personal saga.

John Newton had been what we would call nowadays a wild kid. His mother died when he was very young, and his father, a sea captain, soon despaired of controlling his son. Using his influence, he eventually managed to get John posted as a youthful midshipman on a boat bound for the East Indies. But the boy soon deserted and, through a series of misadventures, ended up in the service of an African slave trader. At this trade John Newton actually prospered, heedless, as he later recalled, of the human misery that brought in the money he so eagerly pursued and spent. He eventually became the captain of a slave ship of his own. If the subject of religion came up, Newton expressed only contempt and scorn; he was, he said, a distinguished blasphemer. And then everything changed. Circumstances arranged for him to be returned to England, and there he was transformed into the Reverend John Newton, curate of Olney. His fame as a fiery evangelical preacher soon spread, and among those attracted to his side was William Cowper, a distinguished poet and his eventual coauthor in the *Olney Hymns*. So, in a real way, "Amazing Grace" is Newton's own life story, his journey from being a lost youth to one who was "found," and from blindness to sight.

But there are always many ways of construing human experience. The stark way, it should be clear, reduces things to what it sees as their irreducible components. Would it help, in the case of John Newton, to know that his return to England was not effected through the direct promptings of the Holy Spirit so much as by a stratagem of his father's manufacture, or to note that what the song calls "the hour I first believed" was, in his case, not an hour out of nowhere, but a certain stage in a far longer transformation, one that was gradual and not sudden? Certainly John Newton would feel justified in answering this question in the negative. Of course he sought to tell the truth about his own life. But what is one to say? Experienced in the depth of the soul, events from the world of the sun take on a different look. What sort of hymn would it be if he had said, sun-style, "I once was lost, but really, I'm feeling much better now—I was blind, but lately my vision has improved considerably"? In the world of the soul, there really are only two options: righteous or wicked, a blessing or a curse. Shilly-shallying is just stalling. Looking back, John Newton, or anyone else who had made his journey, would rightly say that what really happened was what he had described:

> Amazing grace! (How sweet the sound!)
> That saved a wretch like me.
> I once was lost but now am found,
> Was blind but now I see.

ɞ ɞ ɞ

The stark view, I have been suggesting, has something to do with perception itself, with (as John Newton says) seeing after having been blind. It is not like everyday perception. While it focuses on the things of this world, it sees them quite differently; they are turned to strange polarities and primary colors, even cartoonized. This way of seeing may be exemplified here and there in biblical texts, but it is hardly limited to the Bible; the medieval Hebrew poem with which we began, as well as "Amazing Grace" and a great many other religious texts, prose and poetry, share this same vision.

Considered from the outside, starkness seems not only distorted, but *willfully* so; the author, we feel, is being unrealistic on purpose or is, at best, blinded by his or her fervent belief. There is no doubt some truth to this, at times. But to view starkness only in this way is, I think, to fail to treat it with the seriousness it deserves. In any case, I have tried to come at it from the opposite side, to suppose that, on the contrary, starkness is a faithful representation of something real, or something that was real at one time. Indeed, the very fact that it is apparently widespread suggests it may have to do with something basic, something (as I said earlier) experienced in the "depth of the soul." I have not used this phrase lightly. Since Descartes, souls have generally been disdained in serious discourse. But the Hebrew poem with which we began was a poem *about* the soul, after all, and that poem's nighttime journey and its stark vision of the Heavenly Throne are recounted from the soul's point of view. So it might not be irrelevant to ask what the soul is, or was, exactly. More precisely: how can a thing that was conventionally conceived to be most inside a person also have been thought capable of leaving it on occasion—indeed, leaving it every night, according to that poem—and journeying to some point far outside and beyond it?

The author of the medieval Hebrew poem did not invent the motif of the soul's nighttime visit to the Heavenly Throne. The roots of this notion go back very far; to Isaiah's and Ezekiel's visions of the Heavenly Throne, to the biblical night visions of the prophet Zechariah, and to a whole host of postbiblical ascents to heaven. The soul's nightly ascent to heaven is found within the corpus of rabbinic writings in late antiquity:

> Rabbi Bisni, Rabbi Aḥah, and Rabbi Yoḥanan said in the name of Rabbi Meir: The soul fills the body, and when a person is asleep, it rises up and draws life for itself from on High. (*Genesis Rabba* 14:9)

> Said Rabbi Aleksandri: With human beings, if you entrust them with something new to take care of and it remains with them some time, they will return it to you worn out and used. But with God, when you give Him something worn out and used, He gives it back all new. And here is the proof: when a

> worker labors the whole day long, at the end his soul is tired and exhausted, and while he sleeps (since he is tired) he surrenders his soul and it is entrusted to God. But in the morning it returns to his body healthy and renewed, as it is says "renewed in the morning, great indeed is Your faithfulness" [Lam. 3:23]. (*Midrash on Psalms* 25:2)

The soul's nightly journey was a favorite theme of the late medieval *Book of Splendor:*

> A person's soul goes forth from him when he goes to bed, and it ascends on high. . . . The soul that so merits goes up so far as to appear before [the angel Metatron]; it clings to the desire to behold the King's Glory and to tarry in His palace. . . .
>
> While people sleep and so taste the taste of death, the soul ascends on high. And as she stands in whatever place she stands, she is examined concerning the deeds that she has done during the day, and they are written down for a record. How is this? Because the soul ascends on high and gives testimony concerning the human being's deeds and concerning each and every word that went forth from his lips. When a word that the person spoke is fitting, a holy word of Torah or prayer, that words flies up and breaches the [intermediary] firmaments and stands in whatever place it stands until night falls. Then the soul goes up and takes hold of that word and brings it before the King. But when the word is unfitting or is even one of the bad words, an ill word [concerning someone], that word ascends to whatever place it ascends to and the word is immediately written down, along with the sin, against the man. (*Zohar,* vol. 1, 83a [*Lekh-lekha*]; vol. 3, 121b [*Naso*])

The God of Old

The idea that souls travel, especially at night, is found in a great many different cultures and civilizations around the world, and modern thinkers have not had much trouble coming up with a rational explanation for it. After all, people dream at night—sometimes the most vivid sorts of dreams, in which they see places far distant from where they are or sometimes encounter people from far away, even people long dead. How to explain such experiences? To the primitive mind, such an explanation goes, dreaming is not something that happens inside the brain: if a person awakes and has the feeling that he has actually seen remote places or people, then the natural conclusion is that he in fact has. That is, the soul (or mind or spirit) leaves the body at night—this is what the unconscious state of sleep consists of, being without a soul—and travels to remote destinations, only to return in time for the person to wake up. No doubt such an explanation for dreaming is actually presented by various peoples around the globe; yet one should not be too quick to accept this explanation as natural. If it is natural, then what is our current understanding of sleeping and dreaming? That is, how would sleeping or dreaming have to be different in order for primitive man to conclude that all that was happening was that the mind was going into its resting mode, shutting down the senses and the outside world, and, along with that, allowing itself a kind of wandering free that we call dreaming, which sometimes summons up not only the people or events encountered during the preceding day but also memories of places or people seen long ago? What I mean to say is that there is really nothing more natural about the idea of the soul's journey than there is with some other, strictly internal view of dreaming. On the contrary, the idea of the soul's journey points up something fundamental about the very concept of the soul itself, and with it, the stark way of seeing.

In the Hebrew Bible, the soul is not really the hypothetical entity that this word conjures up in English. Instead, the soul is right there: it is a person's great inside, the place of all the thoughts and desires that lie beneath the surface and are thus not visible to the naked eye. (People did not generally associate these functions with the brain in ancient times.) The most common word for soul, *nefesh,* also used to mean "throat" or "neck" in an early stage of Hebrew. It is what the breath and all nourishment travel through once they are inside the body, and thus the word also came to mean, only slightly metaphorically, "appetite" or "desire." More generally, however, *nefesh* designates a person's mind or self, that inner part of a human being that one cannot see from the outside. Another word for soul is *neshamah,* which comes from the common Hebrew root meaning "to breathe" and thus seems to be analogous to words like "spirit," "psyche," *anima, dusha,* and *atman,* all of which derive from words for "wind" or "breath" in Indo-European languages. In all these cases, the soul is what keeps a person going, animates the body from the inside, and thus in some sense is the very source of our vitality.

Normally, something that is so inside ought not to have access to the outside, at least not directly. After all, if we see with our eyes or hear with our ears, it is because these organs are situated strategically on the border between inside and outside and can thus be in contact with both. But the soul (or mind or self) is not. How could something deep inside the body be said to see or hear anything other than through the normal channels? Yet souls were conventionally said to do so, as well as actually to travel outside of the body at night in dreams or to visit the Heavenly Throne. Like breath itself, the soul could leave the body for a while and then return. This motif of mobility (in breathing or in dreaming) was, it seems to me, a way of explaining what was otherwise quite inexplicable, the feeling that the inside-outside border was somehow crossable, that there was some way into and out of the body other than via the senses.

This same inside-outside connection is expressed in other ways as well. Although the soul is the place of a person's innermost being, it is not always said to be identical with the person who owns it. On the contrary, the soul is commonly conceived to come from, or in some formulations even to belong to, God. Thus, the song with which we began asserts that souls are chipped off the Heavenly Throne and reside in human beings only temporarily, as a "handmaiden betrothed" or "what was lent" for a short while. These ideas have deep roots, some going back to the Bible itself. The book of Proverbs maintains that "the soul of man is God's lamp, who searches out his inmost parts" (Prov. 20:27). The idea seems to be not only that the soul is a source of light (a notion also found in the above song), but that God *uses* this light like a torch in order to probe a human being's inmost thoughts. In other words, the soul is a tool that belongs to God, even though it is stored in a human being's deepest recesses. The same idea of the soul's belonging to God is elaborated in many places in the Bible, albeit in somewhat less provocative form. Thus, the soul is "given to" or "put into" or "breathed into" a person by God at birth, only to be "gathered back" or "returned" to Him when the person dies. Between these two events, it is the soul that "thirsts for," "desires," or "delights in"

God, and this too seems to be expressive of its special connection with God.

The soul's nighttime journey ought, therefore, not to be considered in isolation: the journey is, at least in its original context, expressive of the soul's very nature, as an entity inside the human being that, for all its being at his or her very center, is not isolated or marooned there. The inside-outside border is altogether crossable. God is, in Jeremiah's phrase, the one who "probes the heart," that is, who moves from the outside to the deep inside. Especially at night does the border between outside and inside break down. Then God can enter the soul ("You have visited me at night, probed my mind"—Ps. 17:3), or the soul can move in the opposite direction, leaving its human body in order to visit the Heavenly Throne.

ↄ ↄ ↄ

In discussing starkness and the soul's journey, we have apparently strayed far from the God of Old. The God of starkness does not so much enter this world as stand behind it or underneath it, and He does not cross that barrier in order to *appear* to humans. Nevertheless, He does cross it, just as the soul can cross over in the other direction.

In considering these differences, we would be foolish to say that the biblical texts surveyed in this and the preceding chapters are talking about the same thing. They are not, nor is there reason to suppose that they should be. One thing these texts do have in common, though, is the matter of changed perception mentioned earlier. Even what stark texts describe is not, when you think about it, altogether phantasmagoric. In fact, much of what they describe looks, at first glance, like the real world, at least in some respects. But as with the angel narratives, starkness turns out to belong to a different order of seeing. In presenting things the way they do, I believe, all these texts are indeed describing something that had reality for their authors, a way of seeing things that at least some of them knew firsthand (although I am also prepared to admit that sometimes their way of representing this reality appears to rely on set conventions; that is, things are being said in conformity to a pattern established earlier).

What is this reality? Perhaps it would be best to think of the ensemble of all the texts examined so far as comparable to the words of the blind men who, in the old parable, are asked to describe an elephant. The blind man who grasps the elephant's trunk knows one part of the reality, the one who grasps the elephant's leg knows another, the one who brushes up against its side a third, and so forth. What an outside observer can do is take the testimony of each seriously and perhaps, without forcing things, try to see what they may have in common or how they may fit together.

7
The Last Look

Ancient Israel, in common with other peoples of the region, believed in a world of the dead. What exactly went on there is not clear, however. The Egyptians were quite obsessed with their underworld and left us a detailed picture of its activities. The Mesopotamian underworld was likewise limned in some detail. In contrast to both these centers, ancient Israel was rather sketchy about the afterlife. The dead "go down to Sheol"—the underworld—but do not seem to do much once they get there. It was a place of silence. "The dead shall not praise the LORD, none who go down to the Pit" (Ps. 115:17). Nevertheless, the dead can, if need be, be aroused from their sleep.

> Then Saul inquired of the LORD [about an upcoming battle with the Philistines], but the LORD did not answer him, neither by means of dreams, nor the Urim [an oracle], nor through prophets. So Saul said to his servants, "Get me a woman who can communicate with ghosts, someone I can go to and ask

> through her." His servants answered: "There is such a woman at Ein-Dor." So Saul put on a disguise; he got into other clothes and took two of his men and went to the woman's at night. He said to her: "Cast a spell for me with a ghost, and bring up the person I name." But the woman said, "Sir, you must be aware of what [King] Saul has done, how he banished ghosts and soothsayers from the land. Why are you setting a trap for me—to get me killed?" But Saul swore to her by the name of the LORD, saying, "As the LORD lives, nothing bad will happen to you for this." The woman said: "Who was it that you wanted me to call up for you?" "Bring up Samuel," he said. When the woman saw that it was Samuel, she cried out loudly and said to Saul, "Why did you trick me? You're Saul!" The king said to her, "Don't worry—now, what do you see?" The woman said to Saul, "I see gods coming up from the ground." He said to her: "What does he look like?" "An old man is coming up," she said, "and he has a robe on." Then Saul knew that it was Samuel, and he bowed down to the ground in prostration.
>
> Samuel said to Saul, "Why did you bother me and make me come up?" Saul said, "I am in great difficulty: the Philistines are fighting against me, and God has left me and won't answer me any more, even by prophets or dreams. That is why I called you, to tell me what to do." (1 Sam. 28:6–15)

King Saul had indeed, under happier circumstances, banned mediums and soothsayers. But now he was at a desperate pass and so had to get some advice; at the same time, he did not want to be recognized, which is why he disguised himself and went to the woman under cover of darkness. She indeed succeeded in calling up Samuel from the dead.

What can be learned of the dead from this passage? They are asleep. They can be summoned, thought it bothers them to be woken up. (Women, apparently, at one point specialized in this occupation; without having any particular candidate in mind, Saul says, "Get me a *woman* who can communicate with ghosts.") The dead are in some sort of spiritual, one might even say divine, state, so that the medium's first impression of Samuel's arrival, even before she perceives anything distinct, is: "I see gods coming up from the ground." On the other hand, this apparition may not be altogether spiritual—after all, at least according to the medium, Samuel is still wearing clothes. Finally—as the conclusion of this episode suggests—the dead may know the future. I say suggests because one might argue that the fact that Samuel had been a prophet during his lifetime meant that, even in death, he continued to be privy to God's plans. Whatever the case, in the continuation of this passage Samuel tells Saul outright that he will die tomorrow. "Tomorrow you and your sons will be with me [in Sheol]" (1 Sam. 28:19). And so it came to pass.

There is no doubt that ancient Israelites believed in the reality of ghosts and mediums and wizards and soothsayers. After all, trying to contact the dead is, along with other forms of witchcraft and sorcery, repeatedly forbidden by biblical law:

> You shall not practice witchcraft or soothsaying. (Lev. 19:26)
>
> And if any person turns to ghosts or familiar spirits and goes astray after them, I will set My face against that person and cut him off from among his people. (Lev. 20:6)

> A man or a woman who has a ghost or a familiar spirit shall be put to death. They shall be killed by stoning, since their blood-guilt is upon them. (Lev. 20:27)

> Let there not be found among you anyone who causes his son or daughter to pass through fire, or who is an augur, a soothsayer, a diviner, a sorcerer, or who casts spells or consults ghosts or a familiar spirit or inquires of the dead. Anyone who does these things is abhorrent to the LORD. (Deut. 18:10–12)

These laws are not saying, "Do not believe in magic and mediums because that is a lot of hogwash!" They forbid the practices mentioned because, while they may be altogether efficacious, they are abhorrent to God and might cause people to go astray (presumably, to adopt other religious practices that run counter to Israel's God). Indeed, the last passage cited is particularly significant, because what immediately follows it may hold some clue as to the precise purpose of summoning up ghosts in ancient Israel:

> [Moses said:] It is because of these abhorrent practices that the LORD your God is dispossessing them [the Canaanites] to make room for you. You must be pure with the LORD your God. For the nations that you are about to dispossess do indeed listen to soothsayers and augurs—but God did not intend such things for you. For you, the LORD your God will [always] establish a prophet from your midst, from among your brethren—one like myself. He is the one to whom you shall listen. . . . For the LORD said to me: ". . . I will establish a prophet for them from among their brethren, one like you, and

> I will place My words in his mouth so that he tell them everything that I command." (Deut. 18:12–15, 17–18)

The prophet is actually presented here as a *substitute* in Israel for mediums and soothsayers. And how is the prophet's function described? "I will place My words in his mouth so that he tell them everything that I command." One might conclude from this that at least one reason for which people went to mediums and consulted the dead was to find out from them this same sort of thing—namely, what God wanted of them and what He had in store. And indeed, the passage about Saul and the medium begins by saying that Saul had "inquired of the LORD [about an upcoming battle with the Philistines], but the LORD did not answer him, neither by means of dreams, nor the Urim [an oracle], nor through prophets." Saul had tried all the acceptable means of finding out about the future, and it was only when these methods failed that he tried to communicate with the dead—*apparently for the same purpose.*

We, of course, live in a world that denies the reality of ghosts and the mediums and wizards who summon them, and it is certainly not my intention here to argue against the modern view. I presume that most, perhaps all, such mediums are, and were in biblical times, charlatans of one sort or another; in any event, their veracity is not what interests me here. Instead, it is the remarkable way in which the woman at Ein-Dor announces Samuel's arrival: "I see gods coming up from the ground." There was no obvious reason for this turn of phrase—it is not what *our* charlatans say: "I see a figure rising up," "I see someone coming." Modern scholars are as perplexed as ancient ones were to explain the word *ʾelohim* here, which elsewhere in the Bible usually means either "gods" or, when construed as a singular, the God of Israel.* Here, however, it clearly refers to the dead. In Akkadian, as well, the cognate word *ʾilu* ("god") was sometimes used of the dead, as apparently was *ʾil* at Ugarit—but this only deepens the mystery: why? The point is not that one can learn about what really goes on in the realm of the dead from this passage, only that the word *ʾelohim* here, as *ʾilu* or *ʾil* elsewhere, suggests that dead spirits partake of some quality or other associated with God or the gods, so much so that they can be called by the same name. Saul's reaction also seems significant. Perhaps it is merely because of the dead Samuel's former closeness to God that Saul now bows down in prostration when he sees his apparition. But one should recall that this gesture is also the reaction, by now familiar, of various biblical figures when they find themselves in the presence of God or His angels.

ᘓ ᘓ ᘓ

Now surely, this divine or God-connected quality of the dead is not an obscure point, nor is it unique to Israel for that matter. In many cultures, the dead are deemed "spirits," souls that nonetheless continue to exist in some form or other *outre-tombe*. But this belief seems to have taken an extreme form in parts of the eastern Mediterranean and the ancient Near East. In different so-

---

* Indeed, I believe the text joins *ʾelohim* here with a plural verb precisely because the narrator must avoid implying that what he means is God, the singular divine being. It is something less than God but nevertheless godlike or God-connected, "gods coming up from the ground."

cieties there, the dead were actually thought to require food and drink after their death in order for them to continue existing in the grave. It was thus the duty of the living—especially the immediate family—to supply the dead person's needs. The body was just down there, over there, and the person was not *really* dead—just in another, slightly different state of being.

From ancient Mesopotamia scholars have reconstructed the *kispu* ritual, whereby the family went at regular, frequent intervals to invoke their departed relative's name and supply him with the food and especially the water deemed necessary for his survival in the dry world underneath this one. Closer to biblical Israel, at the site of ancient Ugarit, archaeologists have unearthed actual tubes that were designed to conduct liquid to the dead person's remains; the same tubes have been found at Greek burial sites and in the Balkans. Indeed, within the immediate confines of ancient Israel, a similar feeding shaft was discovered in Beit Shemesh. Offering sacrifices to the dead was part of the worship of Baal Peor alleged to have been practiced by Israel's neighbors the Moabites.

This practice was apparently known in ancient Israel as well. It is mentioned in a negative way in Ps. 106:28, "They attached themselves to Baal Peor, ate sacrifices offered to the dead." But feeding the dead is also mentioned—without any apparent prejudicial meaning—in Deut. 26:14; there it is specified that an Israelite needs to declare of the crops he has tithed, "I have not deposited any of it with the dead." In excavations at various places in Judah, archaeologists have found animal bones in various kinds of graves and burial sites, and along with them, bowls, jars, and jugs in which dead people might keep and consume the food and drink that were given to them. All these things attest to the basic belief that the dead remain very much with the living; they required ongoing feeding and caring.

What is particularly striking in the case of Samuel and Saul is that the text is quite explicit that these spiritual beings, like angels or God Himself, were conceived to be capable of breaking through into this world, "coming up from the ground," even wearing clothes. They may not like to be woken up and summoned, but they can be. Contacting the dead, in other words, is another area in biblical Israel where "this world" can sometimes be pierced through by another reality not far off—just under the ground, in fact—but not normally in evidence.

ɞ ɞ ɞ

Where the worlds of the living and of the dead overlap most routinely is not in encounters such as this one, but at the time of an ordinary person's death. In the biblical world, the time of death's approach was often thought to be a unique moment of vision, when a human being could peer into the future. Not always, of course. David on his deathbed exhibits very little vision; in fact, he seems more like a dying patriarch from the world of *The Godfather,* instructing his son as to who exactly is to be eliminated next:

> [The dying David said to Solomon:] "Now, you know what Joab son of Zeruiah did to me—how he killed the two commanders of Israel's armies, Abner son of Ner and Amasa son of Jether. . . . So be smart: don't let him die peacefully of old age. But as for the sons of Barzillai the Gileadite, you should treat them nicely and invite them to your table to eat, because that's

> the way they treated me when I was running from your brother Absalom. Now, as for Shimei son of Gera, the Benjaminite from Bahurim, he once cursed me with a terrible curse, the day I went down to Mahanaim. . . . So don't let him get away with it. You're a smart fellow. You know what to do." (1 Kings 2:5–9)

But David's last-minute preoccupation with his political enemies is exceptional. Most biblical figures at the time of their death are presented as being concerned with (and actually able to see) the future, and not just the immediate future. Jacob summons his sons to his deathbed and says, "Gather around and I will tell you what will occur in times to come." The text that follows (Genesis 49) seems to treat of the destinies not of his sons alone, but of the tribes that will ultimately spring from them generations into the future. "God will take account of you," Joseph says on his deathbed to his brothers in Egypt, "and you shall take my remains up from here [to Canaan] along with you" (Gen. 50:24). He is referring to the time of the exodus, which will not occur for another two generations. Moses similarly says at the time of his death:

> Gather all the elders of your tribes and your officials to me, so that I can recite these words to them and call heaven and earth to witness against them. For I know that you will go astray after my death and turn away from the path that I have commanded you; yes, you will do evil in God's sight and anger Him with the work of your hands. (Deut. 31:28–29)

The "these words" that Moses refers to is a prophetic song (Deuteronomy 32) dealing with events far, far in the future. Nor did this view of things fade with the end of the biblical period. One extrabiblical text to survive from that time, the *Testaments of the Twelve Patriarchs,* is altogether predicated on the idea that a dying person can see into the future. In this text, each of Jacob's twelve sons makes a deathbed declaration to his descendants concerning the future, warning them of the consequences of their wrongdoing.

Can the dying really see the future? If the idea was apparently accepted in ancient Israel (and in some other parts of the world), perhaps it was based less on a successful track record of deathbed predictions than on the notion—attested in Saul's rousing of Samuel's ghost—that the dead inhabit some spiritual world, thus deserving to be referred to as "gods coming up from the ground," and that as such they have access to the future (as Samuel's ghost proves to have). The almost-dead would seem to partake of the same gift, at least in theory if not in practice; they are almost in the adjacent world and so should also have some ability to see what is in store.

But what could make people believe *any* of this? No doubt wishful thinking has always had a role in mortal humans' dogged insistence that the dead live on: surely we all would like to believe that our departed parents or other loved ones are alive somewhere and that we ourselves will rejoin them there after our own demise. Does this not account for the whole thing, then? Nevertheless, it is difficult to explain why these dead souls should be associated specifically with the realm of God or the gods, why they themselves should be "gods coming up from the ground"—and why that realm should offer a view of the future. Surely one could imagine a kingdom of the dead somewhere else—indeed, under the ground or (as some ancient Jews and Christians thought) elsewhere on earth—without holding that the dead who inhabit it were somehow godlike or could see what was to come. True, dead people do rather conspicuously leave their bodies behind with us; in their new existence, they must therefore get new bodies or do without bodies entirely, existing in some other way. Yet Samuel seems to have a body in the passage cited; he even seems to be wearing the same robe he was wont to wear in this world—perhaps this was just an apparition, but the passage does not say that. (Indeed, societies from most ancient times have buried weapons and other tools alongside their dead to equip them for the world to come—there is nothing particularly bodiless or spiritual in this conception of the dead.) So one is left to puzzle over why the departed should, upon returning to this world, be "gods coming up from the ground." Apparently, theirs is a spiritual world, but one that is not far off; that world and this one interpenetrate.

ɞ ɞ ɞ

The matter of death and the nearly dead is thus another one of the areas in ancient Israel where worlds seem to overlap: the border between life and death is not all that absolute. Laws prohibiting mediums and others who can talk to the dead are predicated on the idea that their activity may indeed be effective; true, Deuteronomy asserts that a prophet is the only appropriate figure to instruct human beings about the future and God's intentions, but that is not because mediums *cannot* do so. That same boundary between the living and the dead is crossed by the Samuel when he rises up from Sheol at Saul's bidding, and by the feeding of the dead and all that it implies about reaching across into the netherworld. And is not the same border being crossed in the deathbed pronouncements of various biblical figures about the future? The approach of death seems to provide them with a perspective not normally available: a dying patriarch can see well beyond what ordinary eyes can see, sometimes generations into the future.

At the same time, one should note that the approach of death provides a different perspective on life, a characteristically stark one (it did not take the Bible to tell us this). The deathbed pronouncements of texts like the *Testaments of the Twelve Patriarchs* or the *Testament of Job* or others are not just visions of the future but moral exhortations to espouse righteousness and reject the paths of evil. Often, these are presented in absolute, black-and-white terms. In other words, underlying these texts is the belief that those who look at life in contemplation of its end tend to see things in the stark way that we have surveyed. Indeed, starkness in the Bible receives its fullest expression in books like Proverbs and Job and parts of the Psalter—precisely those parts of the Bible where death looms largest and human life is a paltry thing indeed:

> O my Lord, what is man that You should notice
> him, or a mere mortal that You should take
> account of him?
> A person is fleeting and insubstantial, his lifetime
> is like a passing shadow.
>
> (Ps. 144:3–4)

This *stark* biblical theme of death and the paltriness of human life finds its best-known and most striking expression in Psalm 90. Before considering that psalm, however, a related matter should be mentioned, namely, the connection between this stark theme and something that was also identified earlier as stark (and not as frivolously as may have appeared), namely, the world of animated cartoons. Of course, cartoons are not made by theologians—that is why their way of representing reality is, or should be, surprising, since it is so similar to the severe, stark morality of the book of Proverbs or Deuteronomy. Here too, the wholly righteous square off against the utterly wicked (and the righteous, in the same predictable manner as in the Bible, will always triumph over the wicked). Moreover, all this happens, as in the Bible, in a fundamentally abstract world, a place of primary colors without shadow.

Yet, as far as death is concerned, any connection between the Bible and animated cartoons might seem counterintuitive. After all, it was pointed out that in the cartoon world, no one dies. In the Bible, by contrast, human mortality is often the whole point—it is universal and comes all too swiftly. This difference aside, however, there is a greater element that joins the two, and that is the idea of human smallness. To think of human beings as existing for only a brief while is to look at them from afar and from above: there they are down there, pursuing their silly human projects, but all too soon their little lives are snuffed out. Now this smallness is very much the perspective of animated cartoons. It is why, in fact, human beings are represented in cartoons as animals—so that we can see them from above, as slightly laughable, *small*, and basically lacking individual detail, characterized only by this or that all-important trait. Cartoonists did not invent this approach: it goes back to Aesop and the Bible and the ancient Near East and the ancient Far East (and doubtless elsewhere as well). The idea is to eliminate all the complexity and potentially conflicting emotions that normally characterize our consideration of human beings in order to reduce them to something small and simple and easily grasped—the slow but steady tortoise, the quick but arrogant hare. It is the very distance between us and the animals that allows this reduction, the elimination of all shadow and detail from beings that, on reflection, turn out not to be animals at all but little model humans, humans reduced to a few traits. This of course, also characterizes biblical starkness. Seen from a great enough distance (preferably from above), human beings in the Bible take on the same kind of animal smallness:

> The LORD looks down from heaven to see all mankind.
> From where He sits He observes all those who live on earth.
> Having formed the hearts of all, He can inspect their every deed.
> A larger army will not save a king, nor greater strength the warrior.
> The cavalry will not bring victory, it cannot win by force.
> But God's eyes are on those who serve Him, on those who trust in His kindness,
> to save them from death and to keep them alive in a famine.
>
> (Ps. 33:13–19)

> For at the window of my house, through my lattice, I looked down.

The Last Look

There, among the foolish ones, I glimpsed amidst
the boys a senseless lad,
passing in the street next to her corner, now
striding up to her house.
It is dusk, as day turns dark; nighttime comes with
its shadows.
And here comes the woman out to meet him,
dressed as a harlot, but secretly planning.
She is loud and she is wayward, her feet will not
let her stay home.
A step in the street, a step in the market, she lies in
wait at every corner.
Now she seizes him and kisses him, then with
shameless face she says,
"The larder's full of food—I had to pay my
[sacrificial] vows today.
That's why I came out to meet you, looking all
around—and now I've found you.
Well . . . my couch is spread with coverings,
colored weaves of Egyptian linen.
The bed's perfumed with spices, myrrh and aloe
and cinnamon.
Come, let's take our fill till daybreak and delight
ourselves with love!
My husband? He isn't here. Gone off on some
long trip,
with a bag of money in his hand—he won't be
back till mid-month."
So she leads him astray with her talk, with smooth
words she overcomes him.

> He goes off with her right away, like a bull about
> to be slaughtered.
>
> (Prov. 7:6–22)

This smallness of human beings is part of the whole stark vision of biblical wisdom. We are, from God's perspective, next to nothing. And yet, our nothingness is not decisive. If there is something that matters in human existence, it is precisely those things that are valued by the stark perspective: doing right, avoiding evil, being righteous. It is against this background (since it is precisely from this intellectual and spiritual backdrop that it emerges) that one should view the famous psalm of human smallness.

> Lord, You are eternal; You have been with us in
> every age.
> Before the mountains were born, and when the
> whole world was in its birthpangs, yes, from
> eternity to eternity You are God.
> You send humanity back to the dirt and say,
> "Return, poor mortals!"
> A thousand years seem to You like yesterday, the
> way they pass; they flow by like a watch in the
> night.
> What is made in the morning will soon fade like
> the grass:
> though it sprouts up in the morning, by evening it
> will fade, dried up and withered.
> So do we [too] finish in Your wrath, overwhelmed
> by Your anger.

The Last Look

You put our sins before You, inspecting our
wrongdoing.
When all our days meet Your displeasure, we end
our years like a sigh.
So the length of our lives is seventy years, or if
generously given, eighty—and most of them are
toil and fatigue.
Then it rushes off and away we fly.
No one knows the force of Your wrath—Your
anger fits the fear of You!
Let us truly know the measure of our lives; then
we may gain some wisdom.
Come back, O LORD! How long until You take
pity on Your servants?
Fill us with kindness in the morning and we will
praise and rejoice all day long.
Match with joy the days You oppressed us, the
years in which we have suffered.
Let Your servants enjoy Your creation, yea, their
children Your mighty splendor.
May the pleasures given by the Lord our God be
ours, and may You uphold what is ours—yes,
uphold what is ours.

(Psalm 90)

The theme of life's brevity may be common enough in the Bible, but this psalm is in many ways unique. It combines the stark view of human smallness with a real sympathy for the pathos of that smallness that is not usual in the stark world. This is no animated cartoon; it does not simply look down at us mere mortals from God's perspective. Instead, it presents a mere mortal looking up to God, fully aware of his human smallness but nonetheless claiming the right to be heard.

The psalm starts by evoking the contrast between God's eternity and humanity's short lifespan. You, it says, have always been there, even before the world was created, but we last for only seventy or eighty years. (It may elsewhere have been a commonplace that God is the Creator of the whole world and for that reason eternal, but that thought hardly underlies this psalm's opening: on the contrary, the psalm seems to say that the mountains and the world itself were somehow self-generated, "born," while God stood on the sidelines.) God is in any case important here not for having made the world but for having always been there, "from eternity to eternity."

It almost goes without saying that this very conception of our life on earth, as lasting only a fleeting moment and thus dwarfed by God's eternity, is one with certain obvious affinities to the stark world. That world, as we saw, is one that depicts all of earthly existence as insignificant—the place of sin and all its ilk, where the empires change like seasons of the year and what really counts, the only thing, is a person's stark label, *righteous* or *wicked.* Certainly to think of humans as living an insignificant length of days belongs to this same picture. That there exists some sort of afterlife that follows our brief stay on earth is hardly universally espoused by biblical texts; a great many seem to hold that we simply die and return to dust, or at best to the silence of Sheol that is hardly different from nonexistence. But whatever may or may not come after this world, highlighting the shortness of human life is nonetheless *stark*—it adopts that eerie, otherworldly stance toward the events down here even if it does not specifically hold out the promise of another, more enduring reality.

Psalm 90 compares our fleeting existence to that of grass. This is a biblical cliché (Isa. 40:6–8, 51:12; Ps. 37:2, 103:15, 129:6; Job 8:12–13; and yet more). What is unique here, however, is this psalm's explanation for life's brevity. There is nothing natural about it; instead, we die as the result of human sinfulness and God's reaction to it:

> . . . we finish in Your wrath, overwhelmed by
> Your anger.
> You put our sins before You, inspecting our
> wrongdoing.
> When all our days meet Your displeasure, we end
> our years like a sigh.

Theoretically, the psalm seems to be saying, human beings might go on living for centuries. The problem, however, is that God cannot stand us, or rather, cannot stand our sinfulness. By the age of seventy or eighty, we all will have racked up enough misdeeds for Him to decide that our time is up, then "away we fly."

Given this state of affairs, what is a human being to do? One might think that the psalmist has been, as it were, setting up the Almighty for a plea to overlook our sins: "Lighten up!" But no, not at all. Instead, the text at first asks only that God make us mindful of the brevity of our own existence, since that is the only way we can gain some perspective on life: "Let us truly know the measure of our lives; then we may gain some wisdom." In this (and in other particulars) Psalm 90 is oddly reminiscent of a section of Psalm 39:

> Tell me, O LORD, how long my time is, and the
> measure of my days. Oh, let me know how fleeting
> my life is.
> You have made my lifespan only inches long; for
> You my existence is nothing at all; everyone's is
> like a passing breath.
> So people walk about like shadows and their
> doings amount to zero; they keep earning riches
> without knowing who will get them.
>
> (Ps. 39:4–6)

The same idea is found in Ecclesiastes:

> It is better to go to a mourner's house than to go to a celebration, since the former is how all people end—which one ought to remember while still alive. (Eccles. 7:2)

But an ability to keep life's brevity in mind is not all that the psalmist asks for: he wishes also to be recompensed now for the years of "toil and fatigue" that have characterized his existence so far. "Match with joy the days You oppressed us, the years in which we have suffered." In other words, there is no real remedy for this short life; we must eventually displease God and die. In the meantime, however, we can at least strive to be aware of our life's limits, and hope (and pray, as here) that God will give us a measure of joy in this existence before it is over.

Psalm 90 was not written in a vacuum. It has affinities to the vast wisdom literature of the ancient Near East, a great intellectual tradition that existed even before biblical Israel emerged and whose fundamental outlook is contained not only in certain specific parts of the Bible (principally, as was noted earlier, the books of Proverbs, Job, and Ecclesiastes, as well as a portion of the book of Psalms and various other subunits). In some ways, this outlook may strike the reader as somewhat reminiscent of Greek Stoicism—this is not surprising, since the Stoics' founder, Zeno, was himself of Phoenician stock and his philosophy's basic orientation was in some ways more Eastern than Greek. In any case, wisdom literature is fertile ground for the stark outlook (though starkness is certainly not limited to this literature), and while wisdom's outlook soon became highly conventional and full of clichés, behind the clichés stands a vision that, even today, must strike us as radical, even shocking.

The best way to understand the wisdom world's view of the meaning of a human life might be to compare an individual life to an artist's canvas. We all start off with a blank canvas, an ancient sage might have said, and each of us is, at least potentially, a world-class artist. That is, no one is better qualified than anyone else when it comes to painting his or her particular painting; we each have all the requisite tools and talents. Nevertheless, we will not all produce a masterpiece. The outcome has little to do with the actual subject of the painting we choose to paint: a Cézanne will always be a Cézanne, whether the artist is painting nude bathers or a bowl of fruit. So similarly, with us, it is not really the *subject* of our life that counts. In today's terms, it was great, truly wonderful, for you to get to be editor in chief, or make that astounding discovery in astrophysics, or be so deft at surgery, but in the end, these things are not crucial. And certainly it has nothing to do with all the money you made, since within a generation or two—or three or four at the most—those great riches will all be dissipated. (This is a favorite wisdom theme: as we just observed Ps. 39:7 to say, "So people walk about like shadows and their doings amount to zero; they keep earning riches without knowing who will get them.")

Instead, important reality operates on a different level of things—it is not in the overt subject, but in the little brush strokes, all the little, everyday events and *things* that make up our lives. They may be past in a historical sense, but they are nonetheless present, each one of them, on the canvas, and it is they, taken together, that make up our painting. Life is thus a process of filling in. At first, one's life can be anything, the painting can be anything, and in this is both great potential and nothing solid—nothing is filled in yet. (Thus, "Better the end of a thing than its beginning," says Eccles. 7:8: the project completed is unarguably better than mere plans or potential.) But as each brush stroke fills the canvas more and more, makes it "better," it leaves a little less room for all the other things that might have been. And so life goes on, as the potential becomes actual and the canvas fills up, until it is filled up completely.

It was difficult to get some sense of the whole while the painting was being painted, but now that it is done, we can take a step back and see it for what it is. This canvas is the only thing of our existence that endures. To be sure, it does not endure in any tangible way, since nothing tangible endures in any case. (This is what wisdom texts mean in speaking of a person's abstract "name"—Prov. 10:7, Eccles. 7:1, and so forth.) But it is no less real for being intangible—that is the essence of the stark world—in fact, it is only thanks to its intangibility that it does endure, and it is the only thing that matters. Of course, there are many, many canvases. But that does not change the fact that each of us gets to paint one, and when it is done it is ours forever—it is all that *is* ours, on into howling eternity.

This is, of course, not to be thought of as the *biblical* view of life—as with many items, there is no biblical view, since the Bible says different things in different places. But the view just described is altogether characteristic of biblical wisdom—including, of course, Psalm 90—and, more relevant to our overall discussion, seems to capture much of the spirit of starkness, which has nothing to do with life in its variegated detail, nothing to do with good times or making deals, but only with the sharp contrast of moral opposites and all-or-nothing choices, in a world of primary colors without the sun.

ɞ ɞ ɞ

I have written this book without the usual scholarly footnotes (although I have added a few bibliographical and other notes at the end, both to acknowledge my debt to other works and to discuss a few specific issues in greater detail than was possible in the body of this essay). I have also relied a little more on my imagination than a serious scholar would—in trying to think about what it meant to worship idols, for example, or, more generally, in trying to understand the inner world of ancient Israelites. In the process I have also been guilty of wandering from one part of the biblical period to another and even beyond it, to the middle ages and John Newton and televised baseball games. If I have granted myself such license it is because the object of my inquiry seems to be considerably more elusive, and *thinner,* than the usual stuff of scholarship. It is certainly something that now, at the book's end, resists being rolled into a ball and summarized in a few sentences. I hope this does not sound arrogant, that is certainly not my intention. But it is precisely when it tries to address the most important things—what I have called here the Project—that the usual way of doing things leaves me, I must confess, with the greatest feeling of disappointment. I say this not for the sake of criticizing, but only to try to explain my own admittedly fragmentary and indirect approach. I think the most important thing a pursuer of the Project can try to do is focus on the local and specific, and to aim, as much as possible, at being a good reporter—that is, observing without getting in the way.

The testimony I have assembled from the Bible in the present work is not, of course, of one piece. As was already suggested, the different texts cited might be better compared to the blind men and the elephant—the report of each has to be taken most seriously, even if they can be fitted together, if at all, only tentatively, and by the most active effort of theological imagining. What do the various passages examined say? Their common subject is the way that ancient Israel conceived of God and of God's activity in the world. All along we have observed an obvious gap between the texts we have been examining and the portrait of the great universal deity, all-knowing and all-powerful, found toward the end of the biblical period, on which are based, directly or indirectly, most subsequent understandings of God's nature as put forward by various philosophers and theologians. I am hardly the first to point out this gap. Many students of Israelite religion have charted the course of different ideas about God over the biblical period. Usually these are fitted to some triumphant, evolutionary scheme: Israel started out at a primitive stage, worshiping a specific tribal or clan deity in a fully polytheistic world, then moved up to henotheism or monolatry (the worship of one God while accepting the existence and power of other deities), and from there on to true monotheism, whereby one single, all-powerful deity is deemed to rule the whole universe.

It has hardly been my purpose to try to upset this overview. (True, many present-day scholars have begun to question elements of it, including just how polytheistic the religions of Israel's ancient neighbors actually were—but this is another matter.) What the various readings of this book suggest to me, however, is that the evolutionary approach may fail to do justice to, or even take cognizance of, the implications of the texts on which we have focused. These texts seem to be trying to tell us something, something rather sophisticated, about God's very nature—and that something has little to do with the great, omniscient, and omnipresent deity of later times. To gain some apprehension of their understanding, it is necessary to accept them, as I said earlier, as a kind of report, an account of God's nature written down long, long ago by those whose vision was not, however, shaped by such issues as the one true God's mastery over the whole world. Lest I be misunderstood, I hasten to add that, in saying this, I am not implicitly rejecting postbiblical depictions of what I just called the great universal deity. These too were an attempt to understand things, a model or metaphor. (As I also suggested earlier, however, the fact that they first emerged when they did—at a time when the Jewish people had been exiled to Babylon and were now reminded on a daily basis of their own political weakness, of Babylonian power and the Babylonian gods that were believed to support it—doubtless had no small role in that new conception.)

Scholars have long recognized that the emergence of this great, cosmic deity seemed to leave a void, one filled in subsequent centuries by the appearance of a wholly new sort of angel—not the unstable, fleeting chimera observed in this book, but real divine humanoids with specific names and functions (Gabriel and Raphael and Michael and so forth). They were close, even if God Himself was now remote. And so, in the closing centuries of the biblical period, these angels became a major part of divine reality. The Dead Sea Scrolls, and along with them the small library of books written toward the end of biblical times and known collectively as the biblical apocrypha and pseudepigrapha, offer eloquent testimony to the importance that angels now had in people's daily lives. As God's agents (or sometimes His independent subalterns), angels could intervene in the fate of nations, including that of Israel; indeed, they controlled all sorts of distant or cosmic things, like the weather and the seasons. But they also held sway over things close up, things in ordinary people's lives. Nor were angels necessarily good, or even neutral: wicked angels (including various satanic figures, Belial, Mastema, and others), along with lesser demonic figures, were a constant threat. They too operated on both the grand and the very local scale, sometimes taking possession of an individual's mind or health; they could be countered, more or less effectively, by asking God's help (sometimes explicitly effected through the dispatching of good angels), as well as through pious incantations, hymns, prayers, or curses directed against the evil spirits. All this is to say that, toward the end of the biblical period, God's very remoteness seems to have compromised His standing as the only divine power in the world: in practice, divinity was once again shared. (It is doubtless for that reason that later generations sought to reverse the trend just described: in rabbinic Judaism, for example, angels generally lose their independence of action, and Satan, while sometimes evoked, is likewise radically diminished in importance.)

The end of the biblical period is likewise the time when various ancient worthies, Enoch and Abraham and Levi and Moses and many others, are described as having journeyed to heaven to behold the divine splendor of God's throne. The details of their journeys—and what they saw when they got there—are lovingly spelled out in these late- and postbiblical apocalypses. As noted before, such ascents have earlier roots, yet their sudden proliferation in the closing centuries before and just after the start of the common era seems to be saying something important about the apprehension of God at this time. He does not just turn up anymore, as we saw in Chapter 3; now one must, quite literally, leave this world in order to reach Him. From this develops the mystic's quest, and the fasts, night vigils, and ascetic regime associated with it.

The cosmic God's immensity seems also to have left room for the appearance of various semidivine humans, the godlike man *(theios anēr)* of Hellenistic Jewish writings and various other attempts to promote contemporary or historical figures—Moses or other biblical heroes—to semidivine status. Indeed, does not the eventual emergence of Christianity—in particular Nicene Christianity, with its doctrine of the Trinity—likewise represent in its own way an attempt to fill the gap left by the God of Old?

But I would not like to leave the reader with the impression that the only difference between the God of Old and the later, cosmic deity is one of scale and size, nor even one of divine traits and characteristics. That has not been the point of the preceding pages.

The message that seems to emerge so clearly from the old texts that we have examined concerns, rather, the matter of perception and the *click*. In text after text, the familiar and recognizable things of the world are changed. The human-looking "man" fades into God. In other texts, the world itself looks different, *unreal,* a thing of primary colors without shadows, as people turn to abstract traits and life itself becomes a thing of all-or-nothing choices. If God is not remote in these texts it is because He is, in a sense, just a blink of the eyes away. He is just behind the backdrop, ready to break through. So He hears the victim's cry because He cannot *not;* it is right next to His ears. And He appears, time and time again above the wings of the cherubim, or in a flash, to a sheep farmer, unbidden. Indeed, having already appeared to Moses, He then moves right up next to him and, in that changed moment, can reveal to him fully His true nature.

Once God is big enough and remote enough, however, the matter of perception need no longer have any role. Reality does not have to change in order for Him and us to occupy the same world—after all, there are, at least there *usually* are, so many, many miles between us. So He is "there" and yet somehow controls us "here"; our perception does not need to shift for Him to enter our world because He is already in it. True, for a time, at least, this is not quite because He is omnipresent or omniscient. As was seen in Psalm 139, there is, rather, no spot so remote that it is altogether beyond His ability to *get there before we do,* nor any distance too great for His powers of *discovery* to span. The effect, however, is the same: this God both encompasses the world and can do what He does from afar, which is to say, without the *click* of changed reality, without our very apprehension of the world suddenly becoming very different.

With regard to that *click* and the passages we have examined, one might be tempted to see a process of development at work. Is not starkness simply a more advanced or sophisticated way of apprehending the changed reality of God's presence than the actual visual appearance of some divine humanoid, the angel who fades into God or the fleeting apparition above the cherubim's wings? I do not know the answer to this question, but I am a bit suspicious of an easy yes. It seems to me that both starkness and the fleeting apparition are, in any case, very old, and both ultimately have to do with seeing-that-is-not-seeing. I would therefore prefer to deal with them synchronically, as part of the same elephant. What is certainly undeniable, however, is that in the changed world of the great, cosmic deity, starkness remained an altogether appropriate form of perception; it may not have been necessary, but it certainly was possible and so survived here and there. The apparition of this same universal God in some visual form was far more problematic.

It was, in any case, in the world of the great cosmic deity that a particular aspect of Israel's devotion to its God came to the fore. From earliest times in the ancient Near East the notion had existed that human beings were created to *serve* the gods and do their bidding: one finds the name "Slave-of-[the god] X" throughout the Semitic lands. But it was in ancient Israel that this notion uniquely took root and flourished. Israel's God had made this human bondage altogether central—and incumbent on the whole people: "The Israelites are enslaved to Me," He said; "*My* slaves are they" (Lev. 25:55). And so the religion of Israel became the daily service of God, doing His bidding not only in the limited sense of taking care of His sanctuary and offering Him sacrifices (although that practice is still known, throughout biblical and even later Hebrew, as *ha-'abodah,* "*the* service" proper), but more broadly keeping "all My commandments," all those little rules of home and work, sabbath and holidays, relations with parents and neighbors and officials as well as relations between man and God, that together make up the fabric of Israel's covenant:

> And now, O Israel, what does the LORD your God require of you? That you fear the LORD your God and *follow all His ways,* being faithful to Him and serving the LORD your God with all your heart and soul, keeping the LORD's commandments and laws, which I am enjoining upon you today for your own benefit. . . . Love, therefore, the LORD your God, and always keep what He has ordained, His laws, His rules, and His commandments. (Deut. 10:12–13; 11:1)

Thus, even though a huge, imperial God might be far away, a line of service, of enslavement, connected each and every Israelite to Him; that is to say, each and every Israelite was on His list of employees, and each was in this way brought close.

To say only this, however, is not to tell the whole story, it seems to me. A certain paradox was built into the cosmic God and His service. Huge, remote, and utterly alone, He had unlimited power. But precisely for that reason, He was also more predictable—even, in a way, more controllable. Since the whole world was His, this fact alone imposed on humans a broad perspective, and with it, the feeling of a certain immutable routine. After all, seen from a great enough distance, the world does not change very much, however much individual fortunes may rise and fall. What is more, to become, as Israel eventually did, "a kingdom of priests" (Ex. 19:6), with each individual sworn to serve the Great King like a priest in his or her daily life, while his or her actions were given to the scrutiny of an all-seeing, all-powerful deity, was simultaneously to draw closer to Him and yet to be locked into a fixed relationship. The nature of the interaction would henceforth be clear: You are the only God and I will be subject to You every minute of the day in every way. But "every minute of the day in every way" means, in another sense, never in particular; never in high gear at least, never careening this way and that way out of control. If nothing will change between us, then there will be no eruptions. We have found out just enough: the King is merciful. The God of every minute of every day is an ongoing, regular presence; He is "You," and You are constantly here in our thoughts, even, it is fair to say, in our consciousness. But this same circumstance will explain why You will not suddenly appear out of nowhere, and why You will probably not demand more than You already do (how could You?), which is that we humans walk about in the awareness of You, and pray to You, and try to do what You have said to do, starting a long, long time ago.

ᘓ ᘓ ᘓ

Precisely for that reason, it seems, it is important to glimpse how things once were otherwise; certainly we then may better understand where the present came from. And perhaps also for another reason, somewhat more sublime: to remember that that "otherwise" is, for all that has intervened, not unrelated to what exists in the fullest reality of today. And so, we have seen that shimmering moment of confusion that precedes an angel's fading into God; we have also seen how ancient Israel avoided making images of its God, all the while celebrating His various *appear-*

ances, indeed, setting off a sacred space at which He might regularly be "seen." We have seen how God is not searched for in the Bible but just appears or starts speaking to someone. We have seen the stark world and the sun world—not that they are really separate worlds, but separate ways of perceiving the same world; we have seen the connection of starkness to the soul. Most of the time people in the Bible seem to live in the sun world, but sometimes its fabric rips apart to let the stark world come streaming in—the darkness and the bright light, and the dead, just over there. We have seen that ancient Israel somehow came to believe that it is simply God's nature to hear the victim's cry, that despite all the evidence to the contrary and despite all common sense, this was, in Israel's view, a realistic portrayal of God's essential nature.

This should be enough, and yet I confess that this list still feels preliminary; no doubt other things could be added. Nor, in the larger perspective, is it simply a matter of examining writings from the ancient past. Pursued in the library, the Project can go only so far—everyone knows that. Still, I hope the material and observations collected here may be of some use. Part of the point, certainly, was to say that these texts have always been there, ready to do the talking, if only we are ready to listen. I have always loved those opening words of a certain Chaucer poem, his folksy restatement of a conventional theme of medieval wisdom: "The lif so short, the craft so long to lerne." Later, he said: Go, little book.

BIBLIOGRAPHICAL AND OTHER NOTES

> The philosophers and theologians [of medieval times] were concerned first and foremost with the *purity* of the concept of God and determined to divest it of all mythical and anthropomorphic elements. But this determination to . . . reinterpret the recklessly anthropomorphic statements of the biblical text and the popular forms of religious expression in terms of a purified theology tended to empty out the concept of God . . . The price of God's purity is the loss of his living reality. What makes Him a living God . . . is precisely what makes it possible for man to see Him face to face.
>
> (G. Scholem, "Kabbalah and Myth")

About the epigraph at the front of this book: Somewhat emblematic of my overall theme is the career of this famous description of God in Deut. 33:26–27. Traditional and most modern renderings construe *'lhy qdm,* the "God of Old," as the subject of the second sentence, thus: "the ancient God is a refuge" (JPS), "The eternal God is your dwelling-place" (RSV), and so forth. Suggestive, however, is the New Revised Standard Version: "There is none like God, O Jeshurun, who rides through the heavens to your help, majestic through the skies. *He subdues the ancient gods,* shatters the forces of old; he drove out the enemy before you, and said, 'Destroy!' "

"He subdues" represents MT *m'nh,* whereas *'lhy qdm* is construed as a plural, "the ancient gods" (or perhaps better, "the gods of the east"). This may indeed make better sense out of this admittedly difficult text; in any case, it does encapsulate, in another way, part of the story I wish to tell.

CHAPTER 2: THE MOMENT OF CONFUSION

Scholars have been writing for at least a century about the ambiguous character of angels in some of the passages cited in this chapter. The point on which I focused, however, has been largely neglected—I mean the moment of confusion and the mental fog that seems to accompany it. Although I have separated Chapters 2 and 4, I hope it is clear that I feel that the two phenomena treated in them—the moment of confusion and aniconic worship—belong to the same reality and that they should be considered in tandem.

In writing this chapter, I have consulted a number of works that deal with the general phenomenon of angels in the Bible. Still valuable is the study by W. G. Heidt, *Angelology in the Old Testament* (Washington: Catholic University, 1949), as well as those of Alexander Rofé, *The Belief in Angels in the Bible* (Jerusalem: Makor, 1979), and V. Hirth, *Gottes Boten im Alten Testament* (Berlin: Evangelische Verlagsanstalt, 1975); see also, A. Coudert, "Angels," in M. Eliade, *Encyclopedia of Religion* (New York: Macmillan, 1987), 1:282–86.

There is a vast literature on theophany, starting with Julian Morgenstern, "Biblical Theophanies," *Zeitschrift für Assyriologie und*

Verwandte Gebiete 25 (1911): 139–93, and 28 (1914): 15–60, and Wolf W. G. Baudissin, " 'Gott schauen' in der alttestamentlischen Religion," *Archiv für Religionswissenschaft* 18 (1915): 173–239. Particularly suggestive is the study by J. Kenneth Kuntz, *The Self-Revelation of God* (Philadelphia: Westminster, 1967). Note also Samuel Terrien's *The Elusive Presence* (San Francisco: Harper Collins, 1983); J. Lindlom, "Theophanies in Holy Places in Hebrew Religion," *HUCA* 32 (1961): 91–106. A useful summary of his own and other recent scholarship is Theodore Hiebert's article on theophany in *The Anchor Bible Dictionary.* Mark Smith has discussed one aspect of theophany: "Seeing God in the Psalms: The Background to the Beatific Vision in the Hebrew Bible," *Catholic Biblical Quarterly* 50 (1988): 171–83; note as well the works of his cited below for the chapter on aniconic worship. While I find it difficult to accept its overall premise, Richard Friedman's *The Disappearance of God* (Boston: Little, Brown, 1995) has also helped me think through some of the issues in this chapter. Elliot Wolfson's *Through a Speculum That Shines: Vision and Imagination in Medieval Jewish Mysticism* (Princeton: Princeton University Press, 1994) deals primarily with later material, but it begins with a valuable discussion of the God that is seen—and is itself a vivid demonstration that this seeing did not end with the biblical period.

The matter of appearance and recognition has been treated interestingly by several literary scholars. Terence Cave, *Recognitions: A Study in Poetics* (Oxford, 1988), does not deal with biblical texts at all, but with the recognition scene *(anagnōrisis)* as found in classical Greece and Rome and its varied history subsequently in European literature. Piero Boitani, *The Bible and Its Rewritings* (Oxford, 1999), touches on biblical recognition scenes, especially in chapter 1. Relevant as well is the work of Tzvetan Todorov, *The Fantastic: A Structural Approach to a Literary Genre* (Cleveland: Case Western Reserve, 1973). Obviously, this subject is related to recognition scenes in the New Testament as well, but I have not wished to treat them here.

Biblical scholars have often been reluctant to identify as theophanies the various angel narratives discussed in this chapter. However, in 1960 James Barr wrote a brief article, "Theophany and Anthropomorphism in the Old Testament" (Supplements to *Vetus Testamentum* [Leiden: Brill, 1960], 31–38), in which he strongly argued that the angelic appearance narratives are not to be explained as "a mitigation of the direct anthropomorphic theophany" because (among other reasons) there is simply too much overlap between the angel's words and voice and those of "God" or "the LORD." On the issue of anthropomorphism note also M. C. A. Korpel's *A Rift in the Clouds: Ugaritic and Hebrew Descriptions of the Divine* (Muenster: Ugaritverlag, 1990), a doctoral dissertation directed by J. C. De Moor that usefully compares anthropomorphism and anthropopathy in these two literatures.

PAGE

6 Coming now to the specific passages treated: with regard to the "chief of the LORD's army," see the brief discussion in Rofé, *Belief in Angels*, 2:271–79. As Rofé points out there, some previous scholars (starting with Julius Wellhausen) have seen in this episode an etiological narrative designed to explain the honored place accorded to Gilgal, but he rightly rejects this. Unfortunately, his own suggestion, connecting the passage with the place name Zarethan, strikes me as hardly more persuasive; in any case, my concern was not with the narrative's purpose but with its depiction of the angel. Quite a few recent studies and commentaries have treated the various other angelic appearances cited in this chapter, too numerous to mention; one recent study of Jacob and the angel is that of Stephen Geller, *Sacred Enigmas: Literary Religion in the He-*

brew Bible (Routledge: New York and London, 1996), 9–29; on Abraham and the three men as well as Jacob at the Jabbok, see Lindblom, "Theophanies." Note also the treatment of Balaam and his donkey in A. Rofé, *The Book of Balaam* (in Hebrew) (Jerusalem: Simor, 1979).

16 On the precise affiliations of the passage cited from Virgil's *Aeneid*, see *Iliad* 1:188–222 and, in general, W. Burkert, *Greek Religion: Archaic and Classical* (Oxford: Blackwell, 1985), 186–88. Beyond this epic moment of confusion stands a larger point, well articulated by Robin Fox, *Pagans and Christians* (New York: Viking, 1986):

> No one who knew his Homer could miss [his depiction of] the easy company of gods with men. . . . In the epic poems, the gods mixed with men by daylight, [either] gods in disguise . . . or gods made manifest by signs of their power. When Athena led Odysseus and Telemachus through the suitors' hall, the sudden light from her lamp glowed on the rafters, alerting Telemachus to the presence of a god. . . . It was one of Aeneas's little distinctions that he detected Apollo in the guise of a herald, simply by the sound of his voice. Otherwise, men had to guess. . . . There was no end to the gods' human disguises, as old men and women, heralds, and frequently, young and beautiful people. . . . Did the gods also appear as animals? Occasionally, Homer's gods appeared "like birds," but there is no certain episode when a god turns completely into a bird. . . . Essentially anthropomorphic, the gods stalked the world as mortals, disguising themselves so well that people could never be totally sure that a stranger was all that he seemed. (pp. 104–6)

18 *In that world too, divine creatures present themselves to human beings in such a way that they are not recognized, at*

least not at first—and then sometimes, as with Aeneas and Venus, something clicks: But only sometimes—and this may be an important distinction between Greek and biblical conceptions. Biblical narratives do occasionally describe humans (Jacob at Bethel, Pharaoh and the Egyptians) as not knowing that God is at work—but only *at first*; eventually all is revealed. In classical Greece and Rome, the presence of a god or goddess may go quite undetected.

21 *After all, even the most primitive conception of God (or the gods, for that matter):* The ways that gods communicate with humans through dreams and oracles has been studied by H. W. F. Saggs, *The Encounter with the Divine in Mesopotamia and Israel* (London: Athlone, 1978), 125–52, a book that, despite a lot of subsequent studies, is generally relevant to our overall theme.

22 *Certainly the ten plagues . . . could hardly have been omitted:* In fact, the author of the Wisdom of Solomon does deal with the ten plagues at greater length elsewhere in his book, but here again, the point is to rationalize them: each has a moral lesson to impart to the Egyptians (the folly of worshiping idols; the appropriateness of divine justice). See Peter Enns, *Exodus Retold: Ancient Exegesis of the Departure from Egypt in Wis. 10:15–21 and 19:1–9,* Harvard Semitic Monographs, vol. 57 (Scholars Press: Atlanta, Ga., 1997).

24 *Rather, I would prefer to say that the world in which angels can suddenly appear or disappear is a world in which the border between the spiritual and the physical is not all that clear, or at least not all that respected:* Along the same lines, Karel van der Toorn writes:

> One would be wrong, however, to suppose that the dichotomy between the material and the spiritual world was as natural to them [Mesopotamians] as it seems to us.

> Occasional doubts could not rob them of the conviction that the gods dwelled in the same universe as they did and were to a large extent subject to the same forces and moved by the same reasoning. Our uneasiness stems partly from the opposition of the reality as directly perceived by the senses and a spiritual reality only reached by faith or some sort of mystical experience. This was not how the Mesopotamians conceived of their gods. To them they were the personifications of various aspects of nature and culture, very much present in daily experience. (*Sin and Sanction in Israel and Mesopotamia: A Comparative Study* [Assen: Van Gorcum, 1985], 23)

I whole-heartedly agree with van der Toorn's basic observation—and it is quite well stated—up until his very last sentence. That is, I do not think what he is talking about has much to do with conceiving of the divine in terms of "personifications of various aspects of nature and culture"; in any event, that certainly has no role in the angel narratives we have been studying. Instead, I think the reason is to be sought in a different sense of how the divine and the human, or the spiritual and the material, intersect—and ultimately, a different sense of how *real* the real (that is, sensory) world is. Beyond observing that the ancient Near Eastern sense of things was markedly different from that of our own (or that of the Wisdom of Solomon), I am not sure there is much of a useful nature that can be said. But note in this connection what Paul Veyne writes in his subtle book *Did the Ancient Greeks Believe in Their Myths? An Essay on the Constitutive Imagination* (Chicago: Chicago University Press, 1988):

> These legendary worlds [of Greek myths and medieval lives of the saints] were accepted as true in the sense that they were not doubted, *but they were not accepted in the*

> *way that everyday reality is.* For the faithful, the lives of the martyrs were filled with marvels situated in an ageless past, defined only in that it was earlier than, outside of, and different from, the present. It was "the time of the pagans." The same was true of the Greek myths. They take place "earlier," during the heroic generations, when the gods still took part in human affairs. Mythological *space* as well as time was secretly different from our own. A Greek conventionally put the gods "in heaven," but he would have been astounded to actually see them in the sky. He would have been no less astounded if someone, using time in its literal sense, told him that Hephaestus had just remarried or that Athena had aged a great deal lately. Then he would have realized that in his own eyes mythic time had only a vague analogy with daily temporality; he would also have thought that *a kind of lethargy* had always kept him from recognizing this difference, (pp. 17–18, emphasis added)

"Lethargy" is a key term in Veyne's study, and I hope I am not going too far in suggesting that it is a cognate with the fog in which some of the biblical figures have been seen to exist.

Perhaps in the same connection mention should be made of the ancient temple recently excavated at 'Ein Dara' (tenth to eighth century B.C.E.) in modern Syria. The steps leading up the temple entrance feature the enormous footprints of the god deemed to dwell in it. (For an illustration, see Philip J. King and Lawrence E. Stager, *Life in Biblical Israel* [Minneapolis: Westminster–John Knox, 2002], p. 336). The footprints are sunk into the steps as human footprints might be sunk into mud or wet concrete—but they are many, many times bigger than ordinary, human feet. It certainly required no special insight to see that a god endowed with such big feet would be so tall and so wide that he could not possibly fit inside this temple. (John Monson, "The New 'Ain Dara Temple: Closest Solomonic Parallel," *Biblical Archaeology Review* 26 [2000] 20–35, estimates that on the basis of the stride of these feet, the god or goddess would be some 65 feet tall!) What, then, was being announced in putting the traces of such vastly oversized appendages on the temple steps? I think if one could interrogate ancient worshipers at that site, they would probably say that the deity was indeed that immense (see, for example, Mark Smith, "Divine Form and Size in Ugaritic and Pre-Exilic Israel," *ZAW* 100 [1988]: 424–27 and the works of his cited below for the chapter on aniconic worship). "But how can such a huge god fit in this human-sized building?" you might ask them. Only then might the worshipers concede that there is some difference between the way the god exists inside the temple and outside of it, and perhaps even that a "kind of lethargy" had kept them until now from recognizing this difference.

28 *If not, certainly he must know the truth when the stranger changes his name from Jacob to Israel and explains that "You have struggled with God":* Note the slight but crucial difference here between the MT and the Old Greek (Septuagint). The former says, "You have struggled with God and with man *and* you have prevailed"—referring to the night's fight as one "with God and with man," presumably a God-sent man, an angel. The version underlying the Greek text, however, reads, "You have struggled with God, and with man you shall prevail," that is, you fought with God all night, surely you can overcome any merely human opponent. In considering these two possibilities, one should note that the Greek text form openly states that Jacob fought "with God" (as Hos. 12:4–5 does as well); its mention of Jacob's future struggle "with

men" then becomes an allusion to his impending confrontation with his brother, Esau, who is waiting for him with four hundred men. By contrast, the MT appears to soften the bald assertion mentioned (that is, "with God and with men" might be taken as an elliptical way of saying "a godlike man," an angel), and its "and you prevailed" seems to be telling Jacob something that he already knows.

29 *indeed, "with God" could even be understood as "with God's help":* Such an understanding may underlie the Septuagint's "For you have been strong with God," as well as the renderings of Targum Onqelos, Neophyti, etc.: in any case, it is explicitly adopted by Origen and probably stands behind Wis. 10:12; see my *Traditions of the Bible* (Cambridge: Harvard, 1998), 386–87.

30 *A modern biblical scholar might rightly point out that this narrative is designed to explain the origin of certain things—including the place-name Peniel (or in another form, Penuel) and the name of the nation made up of Jacob's descendants, Israel. Both of these name end in "el," and so in both cases the Bible seeks to explain the name by connecting it specifically with God (El or Elohim in Hebrew):* The etiological approach to understanding ancient biblical narratives was first put forward by H. Gunkel, *The Legends of Genesis* (Schocken: New York, 1964), and has been pursued by many subsequent scholars. I should note that what I intend is not etiological in the narrow sense in which the word has sometimes been used subsequently (that is, principally for name etymologies and the like), but more generally for any story that seeks to explain Israelite institutions like prophecy or the priesthood, Israel's relations with its neighbors—anything, in short, that resorts to past events to account for the way things are now (at the time of writing). Again, Paul Veyne: "Etiology . . . [is] explaining a

thing by its beginning: a city by its founder; a rite by an incident that formed a precedent, for it has been repeated; a people by the first individual born from the earth or by a first king" (*Did the Greeks Believe,* 25).

As for the "el" in place-names like Peniel and Israel, the point is that narratives like those of Jacob at Bethel and Peniel are not only name etiologies, but polemical denials that these place-names, as well as the standing pillar *(maṣṣēbâ)* at Bethel, actually indicate that the sacred site was originally Canaanite, devoted to the worship of El, a "foreign" deity. No indeed, these narratives say, the God in question is our own God, indeed, it is our founder, Jacob/Israel, who gave this place its name. Of course, modern scholars disagree on just how foreign El was; the reader is referred to the brief discussion of the origins of Israel and its religion in the notes to Chapter 4.

35 *That is to say, the real answer to the question "What is your name?" asked of their angels by Jacob and Manoah is nol the answer that they received ("Why should you ask my name?"):* "The [Greek] gods almost never revealed themselves by name when they first met men: only at the end of their encounter did Hermes declare his identity, unmasked, to Priam. Usually, the god himself had to give the first clue, and he conformed to a typical sequence of changes. He would reveal his beauty and show that essential divine attribute, height. He would give off a sweet scent or a dazzling light and might speak in an awe-inspiring voice. His rapid enlargement was followed by departure in a sudden flash" (Fox, *Pagans and Christians,* 105).

CHAPTER 3: NOT SEARCHING FOR GOD

Here it might be relevant to mention some of Kenneth Kuntz's observations *(The Self-Revelation of God)* about the phenomenon of theophany in the Bible. Among other things he notes that the theophany "is initiated by, and only by, the deity himself" (p. 32). Just as we have seen with Abraham, so with other figures as well, there is no initiative taken by the human being or, as we have observed, any special qualification or preparation required of them. Moreover, the human being's reaction to God's self-revelation is never pleasure or satisfaction or even some retrospective sense of honor or privilege; the human response is always one of "fear or dread" (p. 43). Perhaps most significant for our subject: "The theophany is manifested as a temporal event. It is not a permanent reality, but rather it is a momentary encounter that takes place at only particular times. Theophany is transient happening" (p. 33).

PAGE

39 *The* Book of Jubilees *is actually a commentary on the book of Genesis, but a commentary in the form of a rewriting (which was the most common form of biblical commentary in that period:* See my *Traditions of the Bible,* 23–24.

40 *This does not appear to be an incidental detail:* I have pointed out elsewhere (*Traditions of the Bible,* 264–65) that Abraham's question in *Jubilees*—"Should I return . . . ?"—was a way of resolving an apparent contradiction between God's command to Abraham to leave his homeland and the fact that, according to a strict reading of the context, Abraham had already left his homeland and moved to Haran. But this in no way required Abraham's prayer. God might simply have addressed him as in Genesis, telling him initially to go "to the land that I will show you." Then Abraham might have responded with the question that he asks in *Jubilees:* But the people of Ur are asking me to return—should I not go back there, or at least stay here with my father in Haran? To this God could have responded with the words of Gen. 12:1, "De-

part your homeland . . ." In other words, there was no exegetical necessity whatsoever to have Abraham *pray to God* in order to put the words of Gen. 12:1 into a more understandable context. Since there is no prayer in the Genesis original, one is left to wonder why the author of *Jubilees* chose to introduce this new element in his retelling.

45 [*Jacob*] *became, in* Jubilees, *a pious scholar and dutiful son, ultimately the favorite of the same blind father he had cheated—but again, there is nothing of this in Genesis:* See *Traditions of the Bible,* 353–54, 365–66, 368. This may in part represent Hellenistic influence, but I am skeptical; a similar change did occur in Greek writings, but simultaneously or even somewhat later. "Homer had not explicitly linked visions of the gods with moral and spiritual excellence: the gods tended to be seen by friends or favorites to whom they wished to appear. . . . By the Christian era, the 'vision' of a god was attached explicitly to pious spiritual effort. By the mid-second [C.E.], the new art of theurgy aimed to 'summon' the gods by symbols which they themselves had revealed. Its masters distinguished it sharply from magic, because it required spiritual and moral excellence in its practitioners" (Fox, *Pagans and Christians,* 125–26).

45 *All this is interesting, it seems to me, precisely because our age is one in which God is axiomatically remote, a time of "the eclipse of God":* See M. Buber, "Religion and Reality," in *Eclipse of God: Studies in the Relation Between Religion and Philosophy* (New York: Harper & Brothers, 1952), 13–24.

46 *One feature of the Bible that has long been recognized by scholars is the prophetic call narrative:* A commonplace of biblical scholarship; see, inter alia, J. Lindblom, *Prophecy in Ancient Israel* (Philadelphia: Fortress, 1962), 182–97; note also the discussion in Robert Wilson, *Prophecy and Society* (Philadelphia: Fortress, 1980), 171–72. On the eternal ques-

tion of whether the *qātîl* form of Hebrew *nb*ʾ ("prophet") is to be construed as active (that is, the prophet is a "caller") or passive ("the one called"), Daniel Fleming attempted to use newly published Akkadian texts from Syria to argue for an active meaning: "The Etymological Origins of the Hebrew *nābîʾ*: The One Who Invokes God," *CBQ* 55 (1993): 217–24. John Huehnergard argued against Fleming's construction of the evidence in "On the Etymology and Meaning of Hebrew *nābîʾ*," *Eretz Yisrael* 26 (1999): 88–93. The verdict: passive.

51 *The great medieval philosopher Maimonides declared the knowledge of God (which for him was not merely an* amor Dei intellectualis *but a living encounter) to be the goal and highest good to which a human being might attain:* Maimonides, *Mishneh Torah,* Book of Knowledge, 1:1. Isadore Twersky: " 'Knowing God' is both a refrain and a leitmotif of all Maimonidean writing; it is a goal and a means" (*Introduction to the Code of Maimonides* [New Haven: Yale, 1980], 261). An exceptional treatment of the contradictions inherent in Maimonidean monotheism is Kenneth Seeskin, *Searching for a Distant God: The Legacy of Maimonides* (New York: Oxford, 2000), especially 23–65.

51 *"Morning and eve have I searched for You":* For the text, see Hayyim (Jefim) Schirmann, *Hebrew Poetry in Spain and Provence* (Tel Aviv: Dvir, 1954), 1:238. It would probably be wrong to read too much of ibn Gabirol's own philosophical stance into this very public poem, and to do so would be in any case quite beside the point; my reason for citing it is simply to adduce one witness among thousands to a sense of things altogether different from that seen in the biblical world. However, on ibn Gabirol's precise intellectual affiliations: J. Schlanger, *La philosophie de Salomon ibn Gabirol* (Leiden: Brill, 1968).

52 *One well-known motif has it that* prophecy ceased *shortly*

after the period of the Babylonian exile: On the theme of the cessation of prophecy, see E. E. Urbach. "When Did Prophecy Cease?" *Tarbiz* 17 (1946): 1–27. For the reality—that people continued to claim to be prophets, but they were disbelieved—see my *Traditions of the Bible,* 10 n. 8, and the works cited there.

53 *a kind of Hebraic* "Ubi sunt?": The poems cited are indexed in Israel Davidson, *Thesaurus of Medieval Hebrew Poetry* (New York: KTAV, 1970), as numbers 644, 1012, and 6850.

58 *So common is this phenomenon in the book of Psalms that an earlier generation of biblical scholars actually maintained that the psalms were composed to serve as a kind of "poor man's offering":* See P. D. Miller Jr., "Trouble and Woe: Interpreting the Biblical Laments," *Interpretation* 37 (1983), and J. H. Tigay, "On Some Aspects of Prayer in the Bible," *AJS Review* 1 (1979): 363–78.

59 *This explanation is, on the face of it, wrong or at least incomplete:* Some have suggested that ever since Ezekiel's vision of God's departure from His destroyed sanctuary in the sixth century B.C.E., at least some Jews could no longer accept the idea of His residence on earth—and that it was this turn of events that was responsible for God's new remoteness. (See Himmelfarb, *Ascents to Heaven in Jewish and Christian Apocalypses* [New York: Oxford, 1993], 13.) This seems to me most unlikely. That God might no longer choose to inhabit His earthly house (because it had been destroyed, or even because the rebuilt version was somehow inadequate) ought not, in itself, to change His very nature. Let Him indeed inhabit a throne chariot and hover about just above the clouds (à la Ezekiel), making frequent sorties down to earth and appearing just as He did before. In other words, His exile from His house, temporary or otherwise, will not account for the fundamental

change in God's very nature and range of activity that we have observed. This change derives, rather, from the complex of factors observed, principally from the emergence of monotheism and the new status of Israel's God as the one true God of all nations. What is more, the exiled-from-the-temple explanation for God's remoteness does not square with many of the later texts themselves. The author of *Jubilees,* for example, feels that the temple officials of his own day had gone astray and rendered the temple service invalid (*Jub* 6:32–38)—but he nowhere claimed that God had reacted by removing Himself to highest heaven. Instead, God reacted by punishing all of humanity—a punishment that would be reversed when Israel had returned to the proper path. See my "The Jubilees Apocalypse," *DSD* 1 (1994): 322–37.

60 *God thus appears to Moses at Horeb, "the mountain of God"; to Abraham at the "oak trees of Mamre"; to Gideon "beneath the oak tree in Ophrah"; to Jacob at Bethel, and so forth:* The association of trees with God's presence may point to a connection to the *'asherah*. See below, notes to Chapter 4.

60 *Long ago, students of comparative religion highlighted the role of* sacred place *in the religious imagination of peoples around the world:* H. Frankfort, *The Intellectual Adventure of Ancient Man* (Chicago: Chicago University Press, 1946), 20–23; M. Eliade, *The Sacred and the Profane: The Nature of Religion* (New York: Harcourt Brace & World, 1959), 20–65.

64 *One last psalm:* See textual notes to Psalm 139 in my *Great Poems of the Bible* (New York: Free Press, 1999), 327.

66 *God does not know everything in this psalm (again, that He does could easily be said in Hebrew):* On the absence of reference to divine omniscience anywhere in the Hebrew Bible, see the excellent study of Michael Carasik, "The Limits of Omniscience," *JBL* 119 (2000): 221–32. Carasik makes the impor-

tant distinction between knowing per se and the ability to find out, to "probe the kidneys and heart." It is the latter idea that one finds in this and some other biblical texts.

69 *It would be tempting (it has tempted others!) to leave the psalm off on this visionary note:* See the discussion in Geller, *Sacred Enigmas*, 195–97.

CHAPTER 4: NO GRAVEN IMAGES

My whole discussion of aniconism is obviously indebted to the work of Tryggve N. D. Mettinger on this subject. See his "Aniconism—a West Semitic Context for the Israelite Phenomenon?" in W. Dietrich and M. A. Klopfenstein, *Ein Gott allein? JHWH—Verehrung und biblischer Monotheismus im Kontext der israelitischen und altorientalischen Religionsgeschichte*, Orbis Biblicus et Orientalis 139 (Freiburg: Freiburg University Press, 1994), 159–78; "Israelite Aniconism: Developments and Origins," in Karel Van der Toorn, *The Image and the Book: Iconic Cults, Aniconism, and the Rise of Book Religion in Israel and the Ancient Near East* (Louvain: Peeters, 1997), and in particular *No Graven Image? Israelite Aniconism in Its Ancient Near Eastern Context* (Stockholm: Alqvist and Wiksell International, 1995). On the Nabateans discussed by Mettinger (*No Graven Image?*, 57–68), see Joseph Patrich, *The Formation of Nabatean Art: Prohibition of a Graven Image Among the Nabateans* (Jerusalem: Magnes, 1990).

PAGE

71 *These last lines, forbidding the making of images, have been the subject of much speculation among modern biblical scholars:* I have left the discussion of the antiquity of Ex. 20:3 and its placement in the present context for later in the chapter and these notes.

74 *Egyptian religion is scarcely irrelevant to the study of biblical Israel:* This hardly need be said, and yet, in the matter at hand, the importance of Egyptian religion remains a very significant question. The possible connection of Israelite aniconism to ancient Egyptian ideas and practices has been raised by Mettinger and others (just as Israelite monotheism, more generally, has been hypothetically linked to ancient Egypt; see below). Mettinger, while noting the prevalence of anthropomorphic and theriomorphic representations of deities in Egypt, nevertheless asserts that "some of the clearest cases of aniconic cult in Israel's *Umwelt* are precisely from Egypt," specifically in the worship of Aten and Amun-Re (*No Graven Image?*, 49–56). However, he ultimately rejects the idea of an Egyptian source for Israelite aniconism (*No Graven Image?*, 139–40). The detailed study of Othmar Keel and Christoph Uehlinger, *Gods, Goddesses, and Images of God in Ancient Israel* (Minneapolis: Fortress, 1998), might seem to pull in the opposite direction; this survey of the iconography of stamp seals, scarabs, figurines, cylinder seals, and other material excavated at various sites suggests a steady and profound Egyptian influence on emergent Israel, at least in the area of *Kleinkunst*. Much of the material they document consists of clearly anthropomorphic representations of gods and goddesses, although the authors find a decrease in anthropomorphic representation of deities starting in Iron Age IIA, where representation via attribute animals and other entities is documented. In any case, it is not clear what all this might mean for the development of Israelite aniconism. Keel and Uehlinger reject as artificial the formulation of William Dever that religious history is to be reconstructed by identifying "belief through *texts* [and] cult through *material culture*"—material culture, they wish to claim, can tell us a lot about religious belief. No doubt; but it seems

equally dangerous to act as if material finds are unquestionably theologoumena, especially when what they seem to imply about beliefs runs counter to other evidence, including texts. Does every American with a rabbit's foot key chain believe in the efficacity of fetishes or sympathetic magic?

75 *Indeed, the Sumerian word* KU.GAL . . . *was one of the many Sumerian words that passed into Semitic languages, in this case not only Babylonian but Old Aramaic:* Note the divine epithet "irrigation supervisor of heaven and earth" *(gwgl šmyn w'rq)* in the second line of the Aramaic portion of the Tell Faḫariyeh inscription. For the spelling of *KU.GAL / gwgl,* see F. I. Andersen and David Noel Freedman, "The Orthography of the Aramaic Portion of the Tell Fekherye Bilingual," in W. Claasen, ed., *Text and Context: Essays in Honor of F. C. Fensham,* JSOT 48 (Sheffield: JSOT Press, 1988), 16; for problems raised by the script, see F. M. Cross, "Paleography and the Tell Faḫariyeh Bilingual Inscription" in Z. Zevit et al., *Solving Riddles and Untying Knots: Biblical, Epigraphic, and Semitic Studies Presented to Jonas Greenfield* (Winona Lake, Ind.: Eisenbrauns, 1995), 393–404.

On Mesopotamian religion in general, see A. L. Oppenheim, *Ancient Mesopotamia: Portrait of a Dead Civilization* (Chicago: 1964); Thorkild Jacobsen, *Treasures of Darkness: A History of Mesopotamian Religion* (New Haven: Yale, 1976); J. Bottéro, *Il était une fois la Mésopotamie* (Paris: Gallimard, 1993) and *La plus vieille réligion: en Mésopotamie* (Paris: Gallimard, 1998); as well as the aforementioned H. W. F. Saggs, *The Encounter with the Divine.*

77 *these images were not described or treated as mere* representations *of the gods; they were actually said to* be *the gods:* The extent to which ancient Mesopotamians actually believed the gods to be present in their images is a question that has been

addressed by many scholars. In a remark much cited in recent research, Thorkild Jacobsen observed: "The evidence is thus clearly contradictory: the god *is* and at the same time is *not* the cult statue" ("The Graven Image," in P. D. Miller et al., *Ancient Israelite Religion: Essays in Honor of Frank M. Cross* [Philadelphia: Fortress, 1987], 18). However, in the less-cited continuation of this assertion, Jacobsen elaborated on what he meant:

> Seen in this light, a cult statue is a foreshadowing of, and a stage in, a divine presence, a theophany. Here the god can be found, can be approached. If he becomes angry and denies his presence to a community, he lets the cult statue of him be lost or transferred elsewhere.
>
> We must think . . . in terms of a purely mystic unity, the statue mystically becomes what it represents, the god, without, however, in any way limiting the god, who remains transcendent. In so "becoming," the statue ceases to be mere earthly wood, precious metals, and stones, ceases to be the work of human hands. It becomes transubstantiated, a divine being, the god it represents. (pp. 22–23)

In writing this, Jacobsen was seeking, on the basis of his considerable experience, to come to grips with the contradiction inherent in the maximalist identification of a cult statue as *the god*. But certainly one of the conclusions that also emerge from a survey of the evidence is that there existed a continuum of images, which were conceived of in different ways. That is, some items *symbolized* a god's power, or even his presence—a characteristic weapon or tool or animal—but in no way were they thought of as representations of his physical form. Beyond these were statues or other images that were thought to show or evoke what the god looked like, or a form he could adopt, but no more than that. There sometimes existed items that were deemed to serve as actual thrones or plinths for the god, or uncarved pillars or empty spaces for the god to fill or alight upon. Then come representations that were indeed believed to be embodiments of the god, figures in which the god actually dwelt, but with little else specified. Finally one arrives at images that were explicitly said to be capable of seeing and hearing and reacting, granting favor or the opposite, indeed, changing expression or even moving. For the earlier part of this continuum, see Eric Horning, *Conceptions of God in Ancient Egypt: The One and the Many* (Ithaca: Cornell, 1982), who notes "the various representations of Hathor as a woman, as a cow, and as a female with a bovine head. These various iconographic representations are not to be understood as descriptions of the actual appearance or essence of the god, but as hints at essential features of the character and function of the god." About the Sippar cult relief, Jacobsen similarly observed: "It is thus clear that neither the huge sun disk on the stand nor the small one under the canopy is a god—even though the latter is called Shamash in the epigraph. They are merely the god's attributes" ("The Graven Image," 21). For the other end of this continuum, see the passages discussed next in this chapter; also W. Hallo, "Letters, Prayers, and Letter-Prayers," in *Proceedings of the Seventh World Congress of Jewish Studies* (Jerusalem: World Union of Jewish Students, 1969), and my article "Topics in the History of the Spirituality of the Psalms," in A. Green, *Jewish Spirituality: From the Bible to the Middle Ages* (New York: Crossroad, 1986), 1:127–28.

78 *Part of the answer lies in the power that images have, or can have, in everyday life:* See, in general, David Freedberg, *The Power of Images* (Chicago: University of Chicago, 1989).

83 *Similarly, to interact with the god, it was necessary to create a special world—the condensed, time-stopped eternity of the temple—and then actually to give the god a shape, a presence, within that world:* Note Jonathan Z. Smith's concise formulation: "I would suggest that, among other things, ritual represents the creation of a controlled environment where the variables (i.e. the accidents) of ordinary life may be displaced. . . . Ritual is a means of performing the way things ought to be in conscious tension to the way things are in such a way that this ritualized perfection is recollected in the ordinary, uncontrolled, course of things" (*Imagining Religion: From Babylon to Jonestown* [Chicago: Chicago University Press, 1982], 63. I owe this reference to Jon Levenson, "The Jerusalem Temple and the Devotional and Visionary Experience" in Green, *Jewish Spirituality,* 1:60).

83 *A crude, spindly little statue invokes and invites:* Most images recovered from the ancient Near East are in fact rather small, standing ten to thirty centimeters in height. See Mark Smith, *The Origins of Monotheism in the Bible* (New York: Oxford University Press, 2001), 182, and sources cited there.

84 *"When Marduk, leaving the Esagila temple:"* Translation from B. Pongratz-Leisten, *Ina šulmi īrub* (*BaF* 16; Mainz, 1994), cited in K. van der Toorn, "The Iconic Book," in *The Image and the Book: Iconic Cults, Aniconism, and the Rise of Book Religion in Israel and the Ancient Near East* (Louvain: Peeters, 1997).

84 *There is a group of ancient Mesopotamian texts that describe the production of divine statues:* On the *mīs pî* ceremony and related material, see Jacobsen, "The Graven Image"; also A. Berlejung, "Washing the Mouth: Consecration of Divine Images in Mesopotamia," in van der Toorn, *The Image and the Book;* Berlejung, *Die Theologie der Bilder* (Goettingen:

Vandenhoeck & Ruprecht, 1998); Michael Dick, "The Relationship Between the Cult Image and the Deity in Mesopotamia," in J. Prosecky, *Intellectual Life of the Ancient Near East: 43rd Rencontre Assyriologique* (Prague: Academy of Sciences of the Czech Republic Oriental Institute, 1998); and the essays in M. Dick, ed; *Born in Heaven, Made on Earth: The Making of the Cult Image in the Ancient Near East* (Winona Lake, Ind.: Eisenbrauns, 1999), as well as the discussion in Smith, *The Origins of Monotheism in the Bible,* 182–88. Nor were such phenomena confined to the ancient Near East: within the Graeco-Roman orbit,

> Statues were not only the symbol of a god's presence. From the first century A.D. onwards, we know of secret rites which were thought to "animate" them and draw a divine "presence" into their material. Egyptian practice lay at the origin of this, and far into the Christian Empire, papyri still prescribe spells which could be written on a slip and posted into a statue in order to "inspire" it. (Fox, *Pagans and Christians,* 135)

85 *Where exactly the people of Israel first came from is still a matter of scholarly speculation and dispute:* On Israelite origins there is a vast and ever-changing scholarly literature. An outstanding survey of different ideas on this subject is R. K. Gnuse, *No Other Gods: Emergent Monotheism in Israel* (Sheffield, Eng.: Sheffield Academic Press, 1997), 23–61. In previous scholarship, archaeologists understandably started with the assumption that Israel's origins were altogether external to Canaan—either they had entered as conquerors, as the book of Joshua relates, or they had somehow otherwise infiltrated and taken over. Such scholars often fixed on the allegedly distinctive Israelite features of the material culture—the collar-rimmed jar discovered at many ancient sites, as well

as the Israelite four-room house. With time, however, many archaeologists have come to see even these as an outgrowth of earlier, Canaanite features—signs of a basic continuity between the civilization of Canaanite cities that were located in the valleys and the village culture of Israel in the Canaanite hills. For an overview, see I. Finkelstein, *The Archaeology of the Israelite Settlement* (Jerusalem: Israel Exploration Society, 1988). The last word on this question has certainly not been written; I suspect that, in the end, it will not simply be, "We have found the Canaanites and they are us." It may be relevant here to cite Frank Moore Cross's essay "Reuben, the Firstborn of Jacob: Sacral Traditions and Early Israelite History," in *From Epic to Canon: History and Literature in Ancient Israel* (Baltimore: Johns Hopkins, 1998):

> The institutions of the [tribal] league, the twelve-tribe pattern, the institution of Holy War, *ḥerem,* the extension of kinship obligations by covenant, and the choice of a single, patron god, have their closest analogues in the southeast, in Edom and Qedar and in Moab and Ammon. The league god reflected in the onomastica of Edom, Moab, Ammon, and Israel ("nation states") has no analogy in the onomastica of the city states with their pantheons or triads of city gods. These institutions do not stem from urban, Canaanite culture. . . . In short, there appears to be evidence of the importation into the land of Canaan of social and religious institutions and ideology alien to Canaan—but with ties to the southeast. (pp. 68–69)

In any case, the point of my chapter is that, whatever continuities in population existed in the Late Bronze and even Iron Age civilizations in Canaan, Israel's aniconic worship of its God—while such worship may, as Mettinger has shown, not have been unique in the region—says something important, not only about how Israel ultimately came to define itself over against its neighboring civilizations, but also about how it actually conceived of this deity entering and being revealed in the world.

87 *It was the Bible's first interpreters who made so much of the tower:* See my *Traditions of the Bible,* 228–42.

88 *Israel's God, the story says, does not approve of that mumbo jumbo, the complicated temple architecture and all those omen watchers and diviners that function within it:* As many scholars have argued, the earliest phase of Israelite religion featured outdoor altars on elevated platforms *(bāmôt)* at which worshipers sacrificed animals and then ate their flesh. For a developmental history, see R. Albertz, *A History of Israelite Religion in the Old Testament Period* (Louisville: Westminster, 1994).

89 *Some modern researchers have argued that the texts in which this prohibition appears either are not among the Bible's earliest or must have undergone some later revision:* The question about the antiquity of aniconism was raised in a general way by S. Mowinckel, "Wann wurde der J-Kultus in Jerusalem offiziell bildlos?" in *Acta Orientalia* 8 (Copenhagen, 1930): 257–79; for the text of the Decalogue see W. Zimmerli, "Das Zweite Gebot," in W. Baumgartner et al., *Festschrift Alfred Bertholet* (Tübingen: Mohr-Siebeck, 1950), 550–63, and more recently Christoph Dohmen's study *Das Bilderverbot: Seine Entstehung und seine Entwicklung im AT* (Frankfurt-am-Main: Peter Hanstein Verlag, 1985). Dohmen, like his predecessors, takes the position that the commandment is essentially Deuteronomic, although he finds an earlier allusion to such a prohibition in Ex. 20:23. Mettinger rejects the antiquity of even this verse on source-critical grounds (*No Graven*

Image?, 138), but this seems highly conjectural. Moreover, a late dating for the prohibition of divine images is at odds with the evidence of the material culture. (As Mettinger himself points out, the work of Othmar Keel and Christoph Uehlinger has documented a general decline in anthropomorphism in Israelite glyptic art from Iron Age I to Iron Age II B; more to the point is the matter mentioned in our chapter, that to date not a single convincing example of an anthropomorphic representation of Y-H-W-H has been found at any cultic site.) Is it really credible that Israelites at this early date should have *not* been making images of their God without there soon being some reflection of this practice in their programmatic thinking? In other words, it is difficult for me to believe that Israel's *practice* of aniconism, which Mettinger holds to be quite ancient, was not also—precisely because of Israel's sustained contacts with civilizations that did not share it—the basis of theological reflection from early times (Mettinger denies this, pp. 195–96).

A further point: Mettinger's overall thesis sees Israel's programmatic "iconophobia" or "iconoclasm" as having evolved out of a more generalized, West Semitic aniconism that took the form of cults centered (quite literally) on nonfigurative standing stones. Much of the evidence he assembles is quite suggestive, but "West Semitic" is used a bit broadly here. Some of the West Semitic sites he details are actually altogether remote, many quite far to the north of biblical Israel. Certainly there is ample evidence of anthropomorphic figurines of both male and female deities from much closer by—from Hazor and other Canaanite cities, to begin with. (Unfortunately, many of these figurines have not been found in situ, so it is difficult to know what precise purpose they served or how they were used. See William Dever, "The Contribution of Archaeology to the Study of Canaanite and Early Israelite Religion," in Miller, *Early Israelite Religion,* 209–47.) And what of the Edomites and other West Semitic neighbors, with their well-documented anthropomorphic images? Mettinger's association of aniconism with nomadic civilizations such as that of the Nabateans seems more to the point, and it fits well with the biblical evidence (and the much-abused "Kenite/Midianite hypothesis" to which that evidence gave rise in the writings of Hugo Gressman, Eduard Meyer, and others a century ago). See his "Aniconism—a West Semitic Context for the Israelite Phenomenon?" in W. Dietrich and M. A. Klopfenstein, *Ein Gott allein?,* 159–78.

90 *Some scholars now believe that teraphim were actually images of departed ancestors:* Two recent studies have argued on the basis of comparative material that teraphim had a role in ancestor worship and family piety; see H. Rouillard and J. Tropper, "TRPYM, rituels de guérison et le culte des ancêtres," *VT* 37 (1987): 340–61; K. van der Toorn, "The Nature of the Biblical *Teraphim* in the Light of Cuneiform Evidence," *CBQ* 52 (1990): 202–23; and the discussion below of feeding the dead.

96 *Indeed, a few scattered biblical texts seem to imply that "Baal" was another epithet for Israel's God:* On this specific point, John Day, *YHWH and the Gods and Goddesses of Canaan,* JSOT Supp. Series 265 (Sheffield, Eng.: Sheffield Academic Press, 2000), 71–73, and more generally his discussion of Baal worship, pp. 68–127; also Mark Smith, *The Early History of God* (New York: Harper & Row, 1990), 12–26.

97 *It was only at some point in history that a new God—the God of the Bible, known specifically by the Hebrew letters Y-H-W-H—entered the land of Canaan from the south and east, and He became the God of the future people of Israel:* I have in mind here specifically the scenario outlined in Tryggve

Mettinger, "The Elusive Essence: YHWH, El, and the Distinctiveness of Israelite Faith," in E. Blum et al., *Die hebräische Bibel and ihre zweifache Nachgeschichte: Festschrift Rolf Rendtorff* (Neukirchen-Vluyn: Neukirchener, 1990) 393–417, though it is hardly his alone; see the other works cited in his *No Graven Image?*, 168, n. 138, as well as in Mark Smith, *The Origins of Biblical Monotheism*, 272 n. 38, and the above-cited essay of Frank M. Cross, "Reuben, the Firstborn of Jacob," in *From Epic to Canon*, 45–70. Note also Benjamin Mazar, "YHWH Came Out from Sinai" (and the exchange with Cross), in A. Biran, *Temples and High Places in Biblical Times* (Jerusalem: Nelson Glueck School of Biblical Archaeology, 1981), 3–13. That the God of Israel was connected with one or more southeastern sites—Sinai, Seir/Edom, Teman, Paran, Midian, Cushan—is suggested by a good number of ancient texts, including Deut. 33:2–3; Jdg. 5:4–5; Hab. 3:3, 7; Ps. 68:8, 17. Added to this is the reference to *yhwh tmn/tymn* from Kuntillat Ajrud and the Egyptian reference to YHWH "in the land of the Shashu" (a Bedouinlike people near Seir) in an inscription from the time of Ramses II (D. B. Redford, *Egypt and Canaan in the New Kingdom* [*Beer Sheva* 4; University of Beer Sheva, 1990]). For another excellent survey of recent scholarship, this time on Israelite religion, see Gnuse, *No Other Gods*, 62–128, and Smith, *Origins*, especially 142–46; worthy of serious consideration is the controversial presentation of Johannes C. De Moor, *The Rise of Yahwism* (Louvain: Peeters, 1997).

Obviously related to the uniqueness of Israel's religion is the subject of monotheism in the ancient Near East; there is a growing scholarly literature on the existence of different forms of something akin to monotheism among various neighbors of ancient Israel. Among earlier treatments: C. J. Labuschagne,

The Incomparability of YHWH in the Old Testament (Leiden: Brill, 1966). A landmark essay was that of W. G. Lambert, "The Historical Development of the Mesopotamian Pantheon: A Study in Sophisticated Polytheism," in Hans Goedicke and J. J. Roberts, *Unity and Diversity: Essays in the History, Religion, and Literature and Religion of the Ancient Near East* (Baltimore: Johns Hopkins, 1975), 191–200. Lambert argued that individual thinkers in Mesopotamia arrived at a sort of "virtual monotheism," whereby the belief in a single, all-powerful deity emerged from the multiplicity of gods and goddesses. In Assyria, the situation was in some ways comparable: the god Ashur (who was not worshiped outside of Assyria) was, at least in the opinion of some Assyrians, considered to be "all the gods." All this is certainly connected to Mesopotamian kingship ideology; see W. Dietrich, "Der eine Gott als Symbol politischen Widerstands," in his *Ein Gott allein?*, 463–90; also Simo Parpola, "Monotheism in Ancient Assyria," in Barbara N. Porter (ed.), *One God or Many: Concepts of Divinity in the Ancient World* (Casco Bay, Me.: Casco Bay Assyriological Institute, 2000), 165–210. On Egyptian monotheism, Hornung, *Conceptions of God in Ancient Egypt,* traces the history of ancient Egypt's association with monotheism since the nineteenth century (pp. 18–30) but remains skeptical about their validity (pp. 33–60). Jan Assman has staked out a more positive assessment of the idea: *Egyptian Solar Religion in the New Kingdom: Re, Amun, and the Crisis of Polytheism* (London: Kegan, Paul, 1995). On theme of emergent monotheisms in general see also De Moor, *Rise of Yahwism,* especially 41–99, and the other essays in Porter (ed.), *One God or Many?* Relevant, too, are Jon Levenson's reflections on Israel's monotheism in its environment; see in particular "Yehezkel Kaufmann and Mythology," *Conservative Judaism* 36 (1982): 36–43, as well as his classic *Sinai and Zion* (San Francisco: HarperCollins, 1985).

98 *For image making was one item on which Israelite and Canaanite religious practices appear to have differed sharply:* A difficulty inherent in this subject is that of distinguishing between Israelite and Canaanite sites in the earliest period (see the above note on Israelite origins), as well as that of defining image making. For example, at what point did *maṣṣēbôt* (standing pillars) begin to be viewed as unacceptable "images"? Such problems notwithstanding, if the evidence of Canaanite cities like Hazor, as well as more remote sites like Ugarit, is representative, then surely the matter of images was a significant religious *discrimen* in Canaan. See further Dever, "The Contribution of Archaeology."

101 *Philo of Alexandria, the Hellenistic Jewish philosopher of the first century, repeatedly says that Israel was so named because this name signifies* 'ish ra'ah [*or* ro'eh] 'El, *"a man seeing God":* This etymology is probably not Philo's but inherited from earlier Alexandrian allegorists. See further Wolfson, *Through a Speculum That Shines,* chapter 1; Ellen Birnbaum, *The Place of Judaism in Philo's Thought* (Atlanta: Scholars Press, 1996), 61–127.

102 *Time and again, God is presented in rabbinic texts as appearing in human form—indeed, this is one of that literature's most striking traits.* On this subject there has been a surprisingly extensive scholarly study. I should mention two classic articles close to the rabbinic orbit: Morton Smith, "The Image of God: Notes on the Hellenization of Judaism, with Especial Reference to Goodenough's Work on Jewish Symbols," *Bulletin of the John Rylands Library* 40 (1958): 473–512, and G. G. Stroumsa, "Form[s] of God: Some Notes on Metatron and

Christ," *HTR* 76 (1983): 269–88. See also my "In the Image of God?" in *Traditions of the Bible,* 80–82, and the works cited there. On rabbinic writings, see David Stern, "*Imitatio Hominis,*" *Prooftexts* 12 (1992): 151–74); Alon Goshen-Gottstein, "The Body as Image of God in Rabbinic Literature," *HTR* 87 (1994): 171–95; and the rejoinder by David Aaron, "Shedding Light on God's Body in Rabbinic Midrashim," *HTR* 87 (1997): 299–314. Also Jacob Neusner, *The Incarnation of God: The Character of Divinity in Formative Judaism* (Philadelphia: Fortress, 1988); Michael Fishbane, "Some Forms of Divine Appearance in Ancient Jewish Thought," in J. Neusner et al., *From Ancient Israel to Modern Judaism: Intellect in Quest of Understanding* (Atlanta: Scholars Press, 1989), 2:261–70, as well as his "The Measures of God's Glory in the Ancient Midrash," in I. Gruenwald et al., *Messiah and Christos: Studies in the Jewish Origins of Christianity* (Tuebingen, 1992), 53–74; Wolfson, *Through a Speculum That Shines,* 33–51. On the persistence of God's human form into later times, see in general Wolfson, *Through a Speculum That Shines,* and M. Idel, *Kabbalah: New Perspectives,* especially 112–36.

102 *The biblical text seems to stress the faculty of sight itself, almost as if to say, "This was not ordinary seeing, but* seeing*":* This is the usual distinction in later writings, variously expressed: Origen distinguishes between normal sight, through the "eyes of the flesh," and seeing with the "eyes of the heart" (Wolfson, p. 110); earlier Greek sources sometimes spoke of the "eyes of the soul." See E. R. Dodds, *Greeks and the Irrational* (Berkeley: University of California, 1959), and A.-J. Fustigière, *Personal Religion Among the Greeks* (Berkeley: University of California, 1954).

103 *Much of God's appearing in the Bible takes place within one*

particular setting—the temple or sanctuary: See on this Jon Levenson, "The Jerusalem Temple and the Devotional and Visionary Experience," in Green, *Jewish Spirituality,* 1:32–61, especially 37–39; also Lindblom, "Theophanies in Holy Places," M. Haran, *Temples and Temple Service in Ancient Israel* (Winona Lake, Ind.: Eisenbrauns, 1985), especially 246–75.

106 *So the best we can do is designate a special space for Him to appear in, a space that looks empty to the ordinary observer:* One fascinating piece of evidence on this topic is the tenth century B.C.E. cult stand found at Taanakh. It was first described by its discoverer, Paul W. Lapp, "The 1963 Excavations at Ta'annek," *Bulletin of the American Society for Oriental Research* 173 (1964): 26–32, 35–39, and then discussed in many subsequent articles and monographs. The cult stand consists of four levels or tiers. The top tier features a solar disk atop some sort of loping quadruped, perhaps a horse, flanked by a pair of voluted columns. The next tier down has a pair of ibexes, whose legs extend into a "tree of life"; these are flanked on either side by a roaring lion. The third tier down has a pair of what look to be winged sphinxes or cherubim, *but they are flanking an open space in the cultic stand;* and the bottom tier has a naked women with lions. She is apparently the goddess Asherah, consort of El in Northwest Semitic mythology, and it may be that the second tier down is likewise intended to symbolize her presence, since the same lion emblems are again present. In a provocative article, "The Two Earliest Representations of YHWH" (in L. Eslinger et al., *Ascribe to the Lord—Biblical and Other Studies in Memory of P. C. Craigie* [Sheffield, Eng.: Sheffield Academic Press, 1988], 557–66), J. Glenn Taylor proposed to identify the top and third tier down as representations of Israel's God—the top tier

corresponding to the solar symbolism connected with God in some biblical and extrabiblical sources, and the third tier representing the "one who presides atop the cherubim." This would fit nicely with the work of Mettinger and others on aniconism, and with the main point of our chapter: God's presence can be connected with a symbol like the solar disc, but it can be truly *manifested* only by the open space on the third tier. However, some skepticism in this reading of the cult stand is perhaps warranted, see P. Beck; "The Cult-Stands from Taanach: Aspects of the Iconographic Tradition of Early Iron Age Cult Objects in Palestine," in I. Finkelstein and N. Naaman, *From Nomadism to Monarchy: Archaeological and Historical Aspects of Early Israel* (Jerusalem, 1994), 352, 381; Keel and Uehlinger, *Gods, Goddesses, and Images of God in Ancient Israel,* especially 157–60; and most recently the treatment of Patrick D. Miller, *The Religion of Israel* (Louisville: Westminster–John Knox, 2000), 43–45. In this connection I should perhaps also mention the voluminous literature on Asherah as a possible divine consort in the early religion of Israel; see Keel and Uehlinger, *Gods,* 210–48, for discussion and bibliography, as well as Smith, *Origins of Biblical Monotheism,* 222 n. 57. While some scholars have wished to see in the Khirbet el-Qôm reference to Asherah an indication of the existence of such a consort, this understanding was rejected early on by André Lemaire, "Les inscriptions de Khirbet el-Qôm et l'Asherah de YHWH," *RB* 84 (1977): 595–608, and many others; most recently by Keel and Uehlinger, who conclude: "[I]f there is additional mention of his *'asherah,* this is probably not a reference to a personal deity conceived anthropomorphically, but is rather a cultic symbol in the form of a stylized tree, an entity that serves him as an agent of blessing" (p. 401). As others have also argued, there are also good grammatical grounds for rejecting the reading of "his *'asherah*" as referring to a goddess. W. S. Gilbert could say, in correct English, "with his Nancy on his knee," but no similar attachment of a possessive to a proper name in Hebrew has been adduced from the biblical or inscriptional corpus. Especially considering that *'asherah* is also used as a common noun in Hebrew meaning a sacred grove, it is hard to understand why so many scholars have bought into the reading of *wl'šrth* in these inscriptions as the name of the goddess rather than a grove (not, of course, that the grove was not at one time consciously connected to the goddess). For the other side of this argument: William Dever, "Archaeology and the Ancient Israelite Cult," *Eretz Yisrael* 26 (1999; Cross Festschrift): 9*–15*.

CHAPTER 5: THE CRY OF THE VICTIM

PAGE

110 *In some of these passages one finds the same specific comparison found in the above passage: you were strangers in Egypt and did not like the way you were treated there, so do not mistreat the strangers among you now:* I believe the reason why the passage cited begins with the word "and" is that it sees a direct connection between the law of fair treatment for the stranger and the law immediately preceding it: "Whoever sacrifices to any god other than the LORD alone will proscribed" (that is, put to death—see Lev. 25:29). Israelites, of course, might offer such a sacrifice, but apparently the first thought that would come into someone's head after hearing such a statute would be: Oh, that's what those strangers do. This may indeed have been true. Consequently, the Bible hastens to add, "But do not take advantage of the stranger." (The particle

translated as "and" can just as well have oppositive force here, "but.") Strangers may in fact be disproportionately guilty of worshiping other gods, but that is no reason to mistreat them.

119 *If so, are not the above passages really intended only to indicate that God hears all human beings when they pray?:* On the nature and sociology of prayer in biblical times, see M. Greenberg, *Biblical Prose Prayer as a Window to the Popular Religion of Israel* (Berkeley: University of California, 1983).

120 *one of the oddest psalms:* The relationship of Psalm 82 to its ancient Near Eastern environment has been the object of many studies, going back to J. Morgenstern, "The Mythological Background of Psalm 82," *HUCA* 14 (1939): 29–126. Subsequent books and articles are too numerous to catalogue here, but see H. W. Jüngling, *Der Tod der Götter: Eine Untersuchung zu Psalm 82* (Stuttgart: Katholisches Bibelwerk, 1969); Harry P. Nasuti, *Tradition History and the Psalms of Asaph* (Atlanta: Scholars Press, 1988), 108–11; S. B. Parker, "The Beginning of the Reign of God: Psalm 82 as Myth and Liturgy," in *RB* 102 (1995): 532–59; and various discussions of the divine council cited next. This psalm is, incidentally, often ascribed by biblical scholars to the most ancient period, but I do not believe this to be necessarily so; it might just as comfortably be dated to the ninth or eighth centuries B.C.E. Among specific topics evoked, the subject of the divine council has been studied at length by E. Theodore Mullen, *The Divine Council in Canaanite and Early Hebrew Literature* (Chico, Calif.: Scholars Press, 1980); J. C. De Moor, "The Semitic Pantheon at Ugarit," *Ugarit Forschung* 2 (1970): 195–220; P. D. Miller, "Cosmology and World Order in the Old Testament: The Divine Council as Cosmic Political Sym-

bol," in *Israelite Religion and Biblical Theology* (Sheffield, Eng.: Sheffield Academic Press, 2000); L. K. Handy, *Among the Host of Heaven: The Syro-Palestinian Pantheon as Bureaucracy* (Winona Lake, Ind.: Eisenbrauns, 1994); Mark Smith, *Origins of Biblical Monotheism,* 41–53; see also Frank Clifford, *The Cosmic Mountain in Canaan and the Old Testament* (Cambridge: Harvard University Press, 1972).

122 *"He established the borders of peoples to correspond to the number of the sons of the gods"*: In keeping with the Septuagint, Symmachus, Vetus Latina, and Qumran *bny 'lhym;* see P. Skehan, "A Fragment of the 'Song of Moses' (Deut. 32) from Qumran," *BASOR* 136 (1954); Kugel, *Traditions of the Bible,* 12–15, 663–64, 701–3.

125 *It is just in the nature of things that victims will cry out to God and that God will hear them and act on their behalf—indeed, as Psalm 82 implies, the same thing was expected (or ought to have been) of any god in ancient times:* See on this P. D. Miller, *Religion of Ancient Israel,* 12–13, and sources cited there. H. Spieckermann, "Barmherzig und gnädig ist der Herr . . . ," *ZAW* 102 (1990): 1–18, suggested that the quality of divine mercy in Israelite theology may represent the influence of El worship elsewhere: at Ugarit, El was described as *lipn 'il dp'id,* "the kindly El, the compassionate one." It is important, however, to consider the larger picture: however the relationship between El worship and that of YHWH is construed, a mindless transfer of traits seems unlikely. After all, traits of the quite unmerciful Baal have also been found in biblical depictions of Israel's God. More to the point is the fact that the attributes of power, justice, and mercy are part of the standard description of the ancient Near Eastern high god: see Miller, *Religion of Ancient Israel,* 221. I hope I will be forgiven for repeating here an observation from my discussion of Psalm 82, that "it is a

god's duty [that is, *any high god's duty*] to take care of the oppressed, and . . . it is their failure to perform this duty (and not some other duty, such as bringing the rain or causing the flocks to multiply or bringing about victory in war) that most plausibly explains why the other gods were fired."

126 *"My eyes have no more tears":* Translation of Lamentations taken from my *Great Poems of the Bible,* 222–23.

131 *Some ancient interpreters seem to have understood it as a reference to an angel, the "angel of the Countenance":* See my *Traditions of the Bible,* 735–36.

131 *That seems to be what "My Countenance" represents here, something less than God's full presence:* Shmuel Ahituv recently suggested that the use of "My Countenance" here should be interpreted in the light of an inscriptional reference to the Punic goddess Tinnit, who is called *tnt pn b'l,* "Tinnit, the countenance of Baal." On this basis he suggests that the "Countenance" in Ex. 33:14 be identified as a lesser deity, that is, an angel—in fact, the angel who led the people through the wilderness to the land of Israel ("The Countenance of YHWH," in M. Cogan et al., *Tehillah le-Moshe: Biblical and Judaic Studies in Honor of Moshe Greenberg* (Winona Lake, Ind.: Eisenbrauns, 1997), 3*–13* (in Hebrew). My translation of God's sentence, "My Countenance will be going along, *but I will be leaving you,*" is not the traditional one. Most translators since the Old Greek (Septuagint) have rendered the last part as "and I will give you rest" or something similar. (Sensing a problem, the modern Jewish Publication Society translation renders this as "and I will lighten your burden.") From the standpoint of the present discussion, there is no necessity for me to reject this traditional rendering. If God answered Moses' question by telling him that He would "give him rest" by sending His "Countenance" (but not going Himself), then

this was either somewhat euphemistic or evasive—and neither of these would be impossible for God in biblical narrative! Still, "I will be leaving you" is an equally good rendering of the phrase (all translators render this expression precisely as "leave," "abandon," etc., in the nearby Ex. 32:10) and seems far more straightforward.

CHAPTER 6: THE SOUL'S JOURNEY

In writing this chapter as well, I have more than occasionally thought of Paul Veyne's aforementioned work, *Did the Greeks Believe. . . .* It may be unfair to summarize this book in a phrase or two, but certainly Veyne's short answer to his own question would be: they did and they did not believe in their myths, since "the coexistence of contradictory truths in the same mind is nonetheless a universal fact" (p. 84). To put the matter in terms closer to our own experience: we know that the earth goes around the sun and not vice versa—but to what extent does this knowledge manage to shape our own perceptions? Do we not, despite what we "know," actually experience sunrise as the sun *rising* over our stationary world? (I do not mean that the word "sunrise" indicates anything; it is certainly a linguistic fossil; but how many among us watch the dawn and think of what is happening in terms of the earth's movement around the sun?) Similarly, citing Jean Piaget's work on the development of cognition in young children, Veyne writes: "It is no less a commonplace that one believes different truths concerning the same object simultaneously: children know both that toys are brought by Santa Claus and that they are given to them by their parents" (p. 135). Elsewhere, Piaget has written, "For the child, there are several heterogeneous realities: play, observable reality, the world of things that are heard and said, etc.; these realities are more or less incoherent and independent. As a result, when the child goes from the state of work to the state of play, or the state of submission to adult authority to that of self-examination, his opinions can vary strikingly" (*Le jugement et le raisonnement chez l'enfant* [Paris: Delachaux et Niestlé, 1945], 325). What I have tried to do in this chapter is lay out some of the features of the *stark* world and put forth the proposition that this world did indeed have reality in ancient times, as, apparently, it continues to have in our own day. On starkness in general, I have tried to work out here some of the thoughts on starkness in wisdom literature I put down in an earlier essay, "Wisdom and the Anthological Temper" *Prooftexts* 17 (1997): 9–32, as well as in *Great Poems of the Bible,* chapters 6 and 9.

PAGE

137 The liturgical poem with which I begin this chapter, *'Odeh la'El,* is indexed in Israel Davidson, *Thesaurus of Medieval Hebrew Poetry* (New York: KTAV, 1970), number 1570. It is apparently the work of Shema'yah Kasson (or Kosson); my thanks to Professor Joseph Yahalom for this reference. For the historical background, see Yahalom's "Guilt and Blame: Responses to the Spanish Expulsion and Forced Conversion in the Poetry of the Exiles" (Hebrew), in Y.-T. Assis and J. Kaplan, *Jews and Conversos at the Time of the Expulsion* (Jerusalem: Merkaz Shazar, 1999); Kasson is mentioned on p. 278. As for the poem itself, Davidson had noted (vol. 1, p. 72) that it exists in two versions, a longer and a shorter; moreover, the fourth stanza of the shorter version ("He finds her sullied") developed a variant form ("He finds her adorned") and the two were eventually printed one after another in many editions. For the allusive style of early medieval *piyyut* in general, see my article "Obscurity in Hebrew Liturgical Poetry," *Medievalia: A Journal of Medieval Studies* 19 (1996): 221–38, and the works cited there.

139 *the stars that we see in the sky are in fact the visible manifestation of a choir of angels:* This motif is in fact a modification of the polytheistic divine council mentioned in Chapter 5.

146 *"A righteous man's name is a blessing":* I have commented on some of these passages from Proverbs in greater detail in my *Great Poems of the Bible,* 159–80.

147 *Certainly there is something conventional operating here: especially in those biblical writings known as wisdom literature (principally, the books of Proverbs, Job, and Ecclesiastes), the division of humanity into the categories of righteous and wicked seems almost automatic:* See on this B. Otzen, "Old Testament Wisdom Literature and Dualistic Thinking," *VTS* 28 (1974):146–57. This feature is, of course, not exclusive to Israelite wisdom. Nili Shupak has compiled a detailed study of parallel wisdom terms found in ancient Israel and Egypt (*Where Can Wisdom Be Found? The Sage's Language in the Bible and in Ancient Egyptian Literature* [Goettingen: Vandenhoeck & Ruprecht, 1993]). She notes: "Dividing mankind into opposite categories, and placing these side by side in order to illuminate and delineate them, is characteristic of the Hebrew sage as it is of his Egyptian counterpart" (p. 258). In Egypt, one such division found in wisdom writings is between the wise and the foolish; this division is attested (though not widely) in wisdom writings belonging to the Old Kingdom and continues on ("in a less obvious way") during the Middle and New Kingdoms. The wise man *(ḥākām)* and the fool *(kĕsîl, sākāl, 'ĕwîl,* etc.) are certainly well-known staples of Israelite wisdom, perhaps most prominently in Ecclesiastes. However, the opposition between the righteous *(ṣaddîq)* and the wicked *(rāšā'),* so evident in Proverbs, Job, and the Psalms, is far less so in Egyptian wisdom, although it apparently does exist in the instructions of *Papyrus Insinger* (a demotic text whose com-

position goes back to the Ptolemaic period, ca. 300 B.C.E.), where *rmt nṯr* ("man of god"—the same phrase translates biblical *ṣaddîq* in Coptic) is opposed to the "wicked man" *(s3be)*. But what to make of the relative scarcity of this particular opposition in Egyptian wisdom is a good question. It is certainly true that in some biblical instances "wise" is used synonymously with "righteous" (see Shupak, *Where Can Wisdom Be Found?*, 262–63), but it seems to me more likely that "wise" there is being understood as "righteous" rather than vice versa, since in any case *ḥakām* ("wise") does not primarily mean "intelligent" or "discerning" in biblical wisdom writings. It designates someone who "treads the path of Wisdom," that is, the way of moderation and self-restraint enjoined by wisdom texts.

150 *There is another kind of starkness—but I think it is related:* I have in mind here M. Weinfeld's detailed investigation of wisdom themes and vocabulary in Deuteronomic literature: *Deuteronomy and the Deuteronomic School* (Oxford, 1972).

162 *The roots of this notion go back very far: to Isaiah's and Ezekiel's visions of the heavenly throne, to the biblical night visions of the prophet Zechariah, and to a whole host of postbiblical ascents to heaven:* This is a vast topic and the object of a great deal of research. The motif of the heavenly journey is found throughout the ancient Near East—in Greece, Egypt, Mesopotamia, Persia, and of course, Israel. See in general W. Bossuet, "Die Himmelreise der Seele," *Archiv für Religionswissenschaft* 4 (1901): 136–69, 228–73; also Geo Widengren, *The Ascension of the Apostle and the Heavenly Book* (Uppsala: Uppsala Universitets Arsskrift, 1950), and A.-J. Festugière, *La révélation d'Hermès Trismégiste* (Paris: Gabalda, 1944), 313–17. There are, of course, two distinct sorts of journeys, the ecstatic-trance journey to heaven and the soul's final

ascent after death; however, Bossuet sees these as coordinate developments. On the heavenly journey in Second Temple and later times, see inter alia M. Himmelfarb, *Ascents to Heaven in Jewish and Christian Apocalypses,* especially 9–28; D. J. Halperin, *The Faces of the Chariot: Early Jewish Responses to Ezekiel's Vision* (Tübingen: Mohr-Siebeck, 1988); Wolfson's *Through a Speculum That Shines,* 74–124, especially 108–12; and the many works cited there and in Alan F. Segal, "Heavenly Ascent in Hellenistic Judaism, Early Christianity, and their Environment," in *Aufstieg und Niedergang der römischen Welt* II, vol. 23:2 (Berlin: de Gruyter, 1980), 1333–94. Moshe Idel discusses the later ascent of the soul in *Kabbalah: New Perspectives* (New Haven: Yale, 1988), 88–96. Relevant to the rabbinic material I cited is his observation that the theme of the "nightly ascent of the soul is in no way eschatological, nor does it point to a mystical experience" (p. 318 n. 96). Later, the ascent of the soul became a central motif among the Safed kabbalists, chiefly because of their exemplar, Rabbi Isaac Luria, "whose soul ascended nightly to the heavens" (quoted by Idel, p. 92, from Benayahu, *Sefer Toldot ha-Ari*). See also Lawrence Fine, "The Contemplative Practice of *Yihudim* in Lurianic Kabbalah," in A. Green, *Jewish Spirituality from the Sixteenth Century Revival to the Present* (New York: Crossroad, 1987), 64–98.

164 *The idea that souls travel, especially at night, is found in a great many different cultures and civilizations around the world:* See L. Lévy-Bruhl, *La mentalité primitive* (Paris: Alcan, 1922), 98–99; Jan Bremmer, "Souls: Greek and Hellenistic Concepts," in Eliade, *Encyclopedia of Religion,* 13:434. On the soul itself, see the (somewhat uneven) articles on "soul" in different religious traditions in Eliade, *Encyclopedia of Religion,* 13:426–65; also A. E. Crawley, *The Idea of the Soul*

(London: Black, 1910); L. Lévy-Bruhl, *L'âme primitive* (Paris: Alcan, 1927); Festugière, *La révélation d'Hermès Trismégiste* vol. 3, *Les doctrines de l'âme;* W. B. Kristensen, *The Meaning of Religion: Lectures in the Phenomenology of Religion* (The Hague: Nijhoff, 1960), 203–15; and Geo Widengren, *Religionsphänomenologie* (Berlin: de Gruyter, 1969), 427–39. Greek ideas in particular have been studied: Erwin Rohde, *Psyche: The Cult of Souls and Belief in Immortality Among the Greeks* (New York: Harcourt, Brace, 1925); E. R. Dodds, *The Greeks and the Irrational* (Berkeley: University of California, 1951), especially 102–43; David B. Claus, *Toward the Soul* (New Haven: Yale, 1981); and Jan Bremmer, *The Early Greek Concept of the Soul* (Princeton: Princeton University Press, 1983).

As scholars have observed since the nineteenth century, the soul versus body opposition found in later times (and apparently influenced by Greek notions) is not exactly what is found in the Bible. Even in ancient Greece, however, ideas about—and terms for—a person's soul(s) changed significantly over the centuries, overlapping at times (but only in some respects) with such Hebrew terms as *nefesh* and *neshamah:*

> In fifth century Attic writers, as in their Ionian predecessors, the "self" which is denoted by the word *psyche* is normally the emotional rather than rational self. The *psyche* is spoken of as the seat of courage, of passion, of pity, of anxiety, of animal appetite, but before Plato seldom if ever is it the seat of reason: its range is broadly that of the Homeric *thumos*. . . . The *psyche* appears on occasion as the organ of conscience and is credited with a kind of non-rational intuition. . . . *The* psyche *is imagined as dwelling somewhere in the depths of the organism, and out of these depths it can speak to its owner with a voice*

> *of its own.* In most of these respects it is again a successor to the Homeric *thumos.* Whether it be true or not that on the lips of an ordinary Athenian the word *psyche* had or might have a faint flavor of the uncanny, what it did not have was any flavor of Puritanism or any suggestions of metaphysical status. The "soul" was no reluctant prisoner of the body: *it was the life or spirit of the body, and perfectly at home there.* (Dodds, *The Greeks and the Irrational,* 138–39; italics added)

The presence, in Hebrew as in Greek, of different terms for a person's inner being (such as Hebrew *nefesh* and *neshamah,* plus the Hebrew words for "heart," "kidneys," "liver," "innards" [*qrb*], and the like; or, in Homeric Greek, words like *thumos, menos, noos,* and others) has suggested to some observers an earlier stage in human consciousness, when the divided, multifarious self had not yet been replaced by a single, unified "person": "In Homer, then, the soul of the living does not yet constitute a unity. The resemblance of this kind of belief in the soul and that of most 'primitive' peoples strongly suggests that it belongs to a type of society in which the individual is not yet in need of a center of consciousness" (Bremmer, "Souls," 435).

This is an intriguing notion, but a rather difficult one to pursue, at least as far as biblical Hebrew is concerned. It seems quite risky to speculate about the inner reality that the multiplicity of Hebrew terms might reflect; whatever their origin, the various words cited earlier became (and perhaps always were) largely interchangeable. It is in any case far easier to imagine a change in *conceptualization* than a change in the nature of consciousness per se; see also Fox's skepticism on this matter (*Pagans and Christians,* 108). But even if no great sea change in the human mind is represented in the shifting terminology, the idea of a conceptualized disjunction between the speaking and acting "I" and some other "self" is sometimes suggested in Hebrew. Note that Stephen Geller traces what he sees in the Bible as the emergence of a "perceiving, individual self . . . a united human personality for the first time, loving God with all its 'mind, appetite, and force.' Swept away was the division of self into souls of different types that characterized paganism, with its love of multiplicity" (*Sacred Enigmas,* 179). See also my *Great Poems,* 46–53.

164 *To the primitive mind, such an explanation goes:* Closer to the truth is Lévy-Bruhl's description:

> Dreams provide primitive peoples with data which, in their eyes, are equally or more valid than the ordinary perceptions acquired when awake. . . . They are not the victims of a crude psychological illusion. They can perfectly well distinguish dreams from waking perception and they know that they dream only when they are asleep. But they are not in the least bit surprised that their dreams put them in direct contact with the powers that do not permit themselves to be seen or touched. Nor are they more surprised at possessing this ability than at being able to see or hear. (*La mentalité primitive,* 96)

On dreams in ancient Greece, see Dodds, *Greeks and the Irrational,* 102–34. He asserts that, in the earliest period, dreams were taken as relating either objective facts or encoded messages; it is only at the time of Pindar that dreams are conceived to be "something seen by the soul, or one of the souls, while temporarily out of the body, a happening whose scene is in the spirit world" (p. 104). However, this appears to be in conflict with the material adduced by Bremmer, which demonstrates the soul's dream journey even in the archaic age ("Soul," 434). About the soul Pindar himself asserts (fr. 116 B

[131 S.]) that, despite human mortality, "still there is left an image of life *(aiōnos eidōlon)*, for this alone is from the gods. It sleeps while the limbs are active, but while the man sleeps it often shows in dreams a decision of joy or adversity to come." Similarly, Xenophon (*Cyrop.* 8.7.21): "It is in sleep that the soul *(psuchē)* best shows its divine nature; it is in sleep that it enjoys a certain insight into the future; and this apparently because it is freest in sleep" (Dodds, *Greeks and the Irrational*, 135). The dreaming self is hardly divine in Plato; in dreams "our bestial nature, full of food and drink, wakes and has its fling and tries to secure its own kind of satisfaction. As you know, there's nothing too bad for it and it's completely lost to all sense of shame" (*Republic* 9.571). See also John S. Hanson, "Dreams and Visions in the Graeco-Roman World and Early Christianity," *Aufstieg und Niedergang* 23.2 (1980), 1395–1427.

166 *Like breath itself, the soul could leave the body for a while and then return:* I mean to imply that the use of "breath" words for the soul in so many languages may reflect not only the idea that this inside organ is indispensable to the body's functioning (ancient peoples knew perfectly well that this is true of the heart or the brain, too), but that the breath's coming and going, moving from inside to outside, may correspond perfectly to the crossing of the inside-outside barrier (though I concede that etymology is a very approximate tool for reconstructing meaning). Note further that Homeric *thumos* is another breath term, as indicated by the related Sanskrit *dhumah* and Latin *fumus:* apparently *thumos* at one point meant something like "smoke."

Bibliographical and Other Notes

CHAPTER 7: THE LAST LOOK

PAGE

169 *The Egyptians were quite obsessed with their underworld and left us a detailed picture of its activities:* Some scholars have suggested that it reflects a basic Egyptian optimism: things there will be orderly and benign—pretty much as they are here. But note the somewhat different assessment of Klaas Spronk, *The Beatific Afterlife in Ancient Israel and the Ancient Near East* (Neukirchen-Vluyn: Neukirchener, 1986), 86–95, who sees the Egyptian preoccupation with death and the afterlife as an expression of fear—not merely the general human apprehensiveness in the face of death, but more particularly concern about the implications physical death might hold for Egyptian royal ideology (a deified king ought not to die!). Lavish burial rites and the like therefore first centered on the person of the king and only later came to be "democratized."

173 *"Then Saul inquired":* On 1 Sam 28: 6–15, see the commentary of P. Kyle McCarter Jr., *I Samuel,* Anchor Bible (Garden City, N.Y.: Doubleday, 1980), 417–23; Josef Tropper, *Nekromantie—Totenbefragung im Alten Orient und im Alten Testament* (Kevelaer: Butzon & Bercker, 1989), 205–27; Theodore Lewis, *The Cult of the Dead in Ancient Israel and Ugarit* (Atlanta: Scholars Press, 1989), 104–17; Brian B. Schmidt, *Israel's Beneficent Dead: Ancestor Cult and Necromancy in Ancient Israelite Religion and Tradition* (Winona Lake, Ind.: Eisenbrauns, 1996), 201–15. The word *'elohim* in 1 Sam. 28:13 is generally taken as a reference to the dead—whether specifically the dead Samuel or the dead in general is not clear; the use of a plural verb with it seems more designed to *avoid* the singular form (since this might imply that *'elohim* referred to the God of

Israel) than actually to indicate a plural subject. Schmidt's proposal that these were actual "chthonic gods" accompanying Samuel seems without support; Lewis translates "a preternatural being." On the matter of *'elohim* as a term for the dead, note also Laban's reference to his teraphim (apparently images of the dead; see above, notes to Chapter 4) as *'lhy* (Gen. 31:30). A further example of this usage that is frequently cited is Isa. 8:19–20: "If they say to you, 'Go inquire of ghosts and familiar spirits that chirp and moan—for certainly a people may inquire of its *'elohim,* [that is, inquire] of the dead on behalf of the living, for instruction and information'—surely, there will be no dawn for those who speak like this." On this verse see also Lewis, *Cult of the Dead,* 128–32; M. Smith, *Early History of God* (San Francisco: Harper & Row, 1990), 139 n. 10; and Joseph Blenkinsopp, *Isaiah 1–39,* Anchor Bible (New York: Doubleday, 2000). 242. On the existence of necromancy and the cult of the dead in Israel see the above-cited works as well as K. van der Toorn, *Family Religion in Babylon, Syria, and Israel* (Leiden: Brill, 1996). On the overall subject: N. Tromp, *Primitive Conceptions of Death and the Nether World in the Old Testament* (Rome: Pontifical Biblical Institute, 1969).

171 *There is no doubt that ancient Israelites believed in the reality of ghosts and mediums and wizards and soothsayers:* On the significance of the legal material cited, see Lewis, *Cults of the Dead,* 161–62.

174 *In Akkadian, as well, the cognate word* 'ilu *("god") was sometimes used of the dead:* On Akkadian *'ilu* as used of dead spirits, see Saggs, *Encounter with the Divine,* 143–44; Lewis, *Cult of the Dead,* 49–51; also Smith, *Origins of Biblical Monotheism,* 6–7; on Ugaritic *'il* in the same meaning, Smith, *Origins,* 197 n. 25. The word had still broader use in both languages:

Smith, *Origins,* 6; Barbara N. Porter, "The Anxiety of Multiplicity," in *One God or Many,* 242–48.

174 *In different societies there, the dead were actually thought to require food and drink after their death in order for them to continue existing in the grave:* On the *kispu* rite, see M. Bayliss, "The Cult of Dead Kin in Assyria and Babylonia," *Iraq* 35 (1973): 115–25; Schmidt, *Israel's Beneficent Dead,* 28–41. Schmidt observes: "The texts from Mari provide extensive documentation for regular offerings on behalf of dead royalty and other persons of prominence in early second millennium Syria" (p. 27); for offerings in gardens, see pp. 34–35. Klaas Spronk writes: "People gave the dead special things they were supposed to need in their life in the netherworld, especially food and drink. This had to be supplied regularly. In many texts we read of monthly offerings to the dead. . . . One of the things the people of Mesopotamia feared most with regard to the afterlife was thirst in the dry and dusty netherworld. For this reason the provision of fresh water through libation installations connected with the graves was a very important item" (Spronk, *The Beatific Afterlife,* 104–5).

175 *Closer to biblical Israel, at the site of ancient Ugarit, archaeologists have unearthed actual tubes that were designed to conduct liquid to the dead person's remains:* Claude Schaeffer, leader of the original excavation team at Ugarit, was the first to point out the numerous devices used there to bring libations down to the dead in the funeral vaults; see Lewis, *Cult of the Dead,* 97. It is hard to translate such evidence into actual beliefs, however. Arthur Darby Nock observed that such libation tubes were used in Roman times for actual buried bodies but also for ash urns ("Cremation and Burial in the Roman Empire," *HTR* 25 [1932]: 321–59); it seems unlikely that they

were conceived to be conducting necessary drink to the cremated remains! Marvin Pope argued for a Ugaritic locus for the cult of the dead in the *marzīḥ,* in "The Cult of the Dead at Ugarit" (in G. D. Young, *Ugarit in Retrospect,* [Winona Lake, Ind.: Eisenbrauns, 1981]), with reflexes in Israel (Pope, *Song of Songs* [Garden City, N.Y.: Doubleday, 1977], 210–29), but his conclusions have been questioned by others. See Conrad l'Heureux, *Rank Among the Canaanite Gods* (Missoula, Mont.: Scholars Press, 1979); Lewis, *The Cult of the Dead;* and Schmidt, *Israel's Beneficent Dead.* On feeding the dead as reflected in the Bible and in the archaeology of ancient Judah, see E. Bloch-Smith, *Judahite Burial Practices and Beliefs About the Dead* (Sheffield, Eng.: JSOT Press, 1992), especially 105–7, 122–26. David's reference to the *zbḥ hymym* in 1 Sam. 20:6 is widely taken as a reference to the cult of the dead: see van der Toorn, *Family Religion in Babylon, Syria, and Israel,* 211–17.

177 *But David's last-minute preoccupation with his political enemies is exceptional:* It should be noted that the Bible elsewhere presents a more traditional, and pious, set of last words for David; see 2 Sam. 23:1–7.

178 *Nevertheless, it is difficult to explain why these dead souls should be associated specifically with the realm of God or the gods, why they themselves should be "gods coming up from the ground"—and why that realm should offer a view of the future:* see on this Lewis, *Cult of the Dead,* 114.

182 *"The* L*ORD looks down from heaven"* and *"For at the window of my house":* For translation, see my *Great Poems of the Bible,* 40–41, 120–21.

Textual notes for Psalm 90:

184 *"Lord, You are eternal":* This translation seems imposed by

the sense. It may involve emending *m'n* to *m'lm,* but not necessarily; see my *Great Poems of the Bible,* 332.

184 *"they flow by like a watch in the night":* That is, reading *zirmātām* and construing it as the last word of the preceding verse. This exact noun form appears in Ezek. 23:20. To read *zrmtm* as a transitive verb with object suffix (as is usually done) makes no sense—to begin with, it is not a transitive verb, and separating it from the words that precede it make for a nonsensical next verse.

184 *"What is made in the morning will soon fade like the grass":* Redividing the letters as *šnhyh* [*yw*] *bbqr* . . . Once *zrmtm* was cut off from the words that preceded it, *šnh* came to be misconstrued as "sleep" with the next two letters, *yh,* misread as the copula "to be," to which a scribe then added the *yw* as the full spelling.

184 *"Though it sprouts up in the morning, by evening it will fade, dried up and withered":* Great effort has been spent in trying to justify this line's apparent assertion that grass sprouts up, fades, and withers *while it is still morning,* whereas common sense (and the biblical cliché elsewhere) would have the withering, which corresponds to death, take place in the evening. In truth, it is only necessary to realize that this is a three-part line; all difficulty disappears and the preceding line also comes into clearer focus (that is, *bbqr* ends the first clause, *kḥṣyr* begins the next).

185 *"Then it rushes off and away we fly":* Reading *k*[*y*] *ygz ḥyš* might be preferable, but the MT adequately carries the sense.

185 *"No one knows the force of Your wrath—Your anger fits the fear of You!":* "No one" is the real sense of "who?" in such questions, "nothing" the true sense of "what?" and so forth. See my *Idea of Biblical Poetry* (New Haven: Yale, 1981), 7.

185 *"Let us truly know the measure of our lives; then we may gain some wisdom":* The latter part of the verse has always been a problem ("that we may gain a wise heart" [NRSV] or ". . . obtain a wise heart" [JPS]—but *nb'* does not mean "gain" or "obtain"). Perhaps the reading "and may we enter the gate of wisdom *[nb' lbb ḥkmh]*" is not to be rejected. Although *bab* ("gate," "portal") is not otherwise attested in biblical Hebrew, it did make its way into Aramaic.

194 *The Dead Sea Scrolls, and along with them the small library of books . . . known collectively as the biblical apocrypha and pseudepigrapha, offer eloquent testimony to the importance that angels now had in people's daily lives:* See the general surveys on angels cited in connection with Chapter 2, as well as M. J. Davidson, *Angels at Qumran*, JSOP Supplement Series II (Sheffield, Eng.: JSOT Press, 1992), and S. Olyan, *A Thousand Thousand Served Him* (Tübingen: Mohr, 1993); also J. Kugel, "4Q369 'Prayer of Enosh' and Ancient Biblical Interpretation," *Dead Sea Discoveries* 5 (1998), especially 134–36. On demons, magic, and exorcism in Second Temple times there is a vast secondary literature, much of it focusing on the New Testament. See, recently, Esther Eshel, "Demonology in Palestine During the Second Temple Period" (Ph.D. dissertation, Hebrew University, 1999); also F. Bovon, "Miracles, magie et guérison dans les actes apocryphes des apôtres." *Journal of Early Christian Studies* 3 (1995): 245–49; on the place of Satan in early Christianity, S. R. Garrett, *The Demise of the Devil: Magic and the Demonic in Luke's Writings* (Minneapolis: Fortress, 1989).

195 *The cosmic God's immensity seems also to have left room for the appearance of various semidivine humans, the godlike man* (theios anēr) *of Hellenistic Jewish writings:* To be sure, the *theios anēr* is a much older concept; I mean to refer simply

to its particular manifestation in late Second Temple Judaism. See my *Traditions of the Bible,* 544–46, 560–61; for possible shamanistic influences on its early development, see Dodds, *Greeks and the Irrational,* 141–42.

197 *From earliest times in the ancient Near East the notion had existed that human beings were created to* serve *the gods and do their bidding:* Most clearly in a cultic sense: "It is the *communis opinio* of Sumerian and Babylonian literature that the human race was created solely to serve the gods by providing their food and drink" (W. G. Lambert, "Donations of Food and Drink to the Gods in Ancient Mesopotamia," in J. Quaegebeur [ed.], *Ritual and Sacrifice in the Ancient Near East* [Louvain: Katholieke Universiteit], 198). Israel's God did not disdain cultic service, but His service went beyond the priesthood and temple service per se; it ultimately included all Israelites.

ACKNOWLEDGEMENTS

My thanks to the many friends who have read drafts of this book and offered their comments, and in particular to Professors Peter Machinist, Lawrence Rhu, and Lawrence Stager for advice on specific aspects of this study. I am likewise indebted to Bruce Nichols, Carol de Onís, and the staff of the Free Press, as well as to my literary agent, Ellen Geiger, for their help in seeing the book through to publication.

SCRIPTURAL INDEX

Hebrew Bible

Scriptural Index

Scriptural Index

Scriptural Index

SUBJECT INDEX

Subject Index

Subject Index

Subject Index

Subject Index

Subject Index

Subject Index

Subject Index

Subject Index

Subject Index

ABOUT THE AUTHOR

James L. Kugel is Starr Professor of Hebrew Literature at Harvard University and Visiting Professor of Bible Studies at Bar-Ilan University in Israel. He is the author of a number of books of biblical scholarship, including *The Great Poems of the Bible* (1999) and *The Bible As It Was* (1997). In 2001, Kugel was awarded the prestigious Grawemeyer Prize in Religion. He divides his time between Jerusalem, Israel, and Cambridge, Massachusetts.